Kansas City Quiltmakers
PORTRAITS & PATTERNS

By Doug Worgul

Photography by Jeanel Drake

Kansas City Star Books

Table of Contents

The Quilter's Quarters, LEAVENWORTH, KANSAS 4
WHAT TO DO AND SEE *in Leavenworth* 7

Quilter's Station, LEE'S SUMMIT, MISSOURI 14
WHAT TO DO AND SEE *in Lee's Summit*....................18

Kansas City, A QUILTING CAPITAL 24
WHAT TO DO AND SEE *in Kansas City* 30

Jeanne Poore, WINNING COACH 36

Prairie Point, SHAWNEE, KANSAS 44
WHAT TO DO AND SEE *in Shawnee* 48

Liberty Quilt Shop, LIBERTY, MISSOURI 54
WHAT TO DO AND SEE *in Liberty* 58

Showcase of Quilts 64

Kansas City Quiltmakers
Portraits and Patterns

Written and edited by Doug Worgul
Photography by Jeanel Drake
Book design and production by River City Studio
Contributing writer, Lori Wilson
Quilting consultant, Edie McGinnis

Published by KANSAS CITY STAR BOOKS
1729 Grand Boulevard
Kansas City, Missouri, USA 64108

First edition
Library of Congress Control Number: 2001118747
ISBN: 0-9712920-3-5

Printed in the United States of America
By Walsworth Publishing Co.

To order copies call StarInfo, (816) 234-4636

For more information about this and other fine
books from Kansas City Star Books visit our
Web site at www.kcstar.com or visit
www.pickledish.com.

Kansas City Quiltmakers
PORTRAITS & PATTERNS

As much as its music, its food, its cows, and its rootin' tootin' past, quilting is a part of Kansas City's identity. And its a part of its heritage that women can claim as their own.

There are hundreds, perhaps thousands, of quilters in the Kansas City area. Serving these quilters are over a dozen quilt shops. Of these we've selected five quilters and four quilt shops to profile in this book.

For that reason we cannot claim that this book is comprehensive. But if we had selected fifty or five hundred quilters to include in these pages, it would not have been any more complete. Because every quilter's story is, of course, unique. So, though it is not comprehensive, it is, we hope, representative.

The quilters whose portraits appear in this book represent the passion, skill, creativity, dedication and generosity characteristic of Kansas City's quilters. The quilt shops profiled here represent the quality, hospitality, service, selection, and commitment to the craft characteristic of Kansas City's quilt shops.

We picked these five quilters for a very specific reason. In 1999, when The Kansas City Star first reintroduced its legendary Star quilt patterns, we sought the support of area quilt shops. Four stepped forward and have since become our partners in telling the story of the Star patterns. Four of the women this book is about are the owners of these four shops. The fifth is a respected quilt teacher who has also helped spread the word about the Star patterns.

Finally, but perhaps most importantly, there are included in this book directions and templates for five quilts and 13 variations made by our quiltmakers from classic Kansas City Star quilt patterns.

Thanks to Rita Briner, Julie Kiffin, Carol Kirchhoff, Vonda Nelson, Jeanne Poore, and Jerry Stube for their cooperation, counsel, and patience. While this book was being written, family members of three of the five women whose stories are told here faced significant, even life threatening, health problems. The strength of character and faith these women showed during these trials continues to be an inspiration to me.

Thanks to Jeanel Drake for her outstanding photography, to River City Studio for their fine book design, and to Lori Wilson for her research and writing assistance. And special thanks to Edie McGinnis for her editing, expertise, and guidance.

Doug Worgul
Kansas City
September 2001

The Quilter's Quarters
LEAVENWORTH, KANSAS

*J*erry Stube is a southern belle transplanted to the northern plains of Kansas. She's everything you'd expect of a proud daughter of the South. Gracious. Flirtatious. Strong willed and tenderhearted.

Jerry owns The Quilter's Quarters, which is located in an old bank building in the historic and surprisingly vital downtown shopping district of Leavenworth, Kansas.

She was born in Alabama in 1946. Her father was a salesman and moved his family around a lot as Jerry was growing up. To help make ends meet, Jerry's mother made clothes for her family and that's how Jerry learned to sew.

"I can't remember a time when I didn't have a needle in my hand," she says. "Sewing was just expected of girls back then. So my sisters and I learned how and I've been in stitches ever since."

And as you might expect in a household of seamstresses, Jerry says she grew up well acquainted with quilts. "Quilts were always a part of my environment, she recalls. "As we were growing up they were just a part of our life."

Jerry claims she was "morbidly shy" as a girl. If so, she has since fully recovered from the condition. These days she greets her customers with warm hugs and hearty laughter, as if each were a long lost cousin.

Jerry arrived in Leavenworth the way many of its citizens have — in the Army. Actually, it was her husband, Jack, to whom she's been married since 1972, who was in the Army. But the Army couldn't have been much more a part of Jerry's life and livelihood if she herself had been enlisted. The Army employed her, as a civilian, but more than that it, to a large extent, defined her.

THE QUILTER'S QUARTERS
219 DELAWARE STREET
LEAVENWORTH, KANSAS 66048
(913) 651-6510
WEB ADDRESS: WWW.QUILTERSQTRS.COM
E-MAIL: QUILTERSQTRS@LVNWORTH.COM
ESTABLISHED IN 1996
OVER 2000 BOLTS OF FABRIC
10 EMPLOYEES

LEAVENWORTH

"I loved the Army life and being an Army wife," she says. "It was such a big part of my identity. When Jack retired, I had a harder time making the transition to civilian life than he did."

It was in 1968 that Jerry got a job as a patient representative at an Army hospital at Fort Jackson, South Carolina. She says that witnessing the physical and emotional pain that accompanies injury and illness deepened her empathy and strengthened her character and her faith.

"But here I am. And I learned something through all this. There are no 'bad hair days'. If you've got hair, it's a good day."

Ironically, learning that she had cancer was the single most important factor in deciding to open The Quilter's Quarters. "It felt like God was directing me to this place," she recalls. "To touch as many lives as I can with this gift of quilting."

Rita Swann, a customer and friend believes Jerry has created a unique environment at The Quilter's

There's something about quilting that focuses the mind and quiets the soul."

Quilting is a way that women can make a record of certain events or times in their lives, Jerry explains. And she tells a story to illustrate her point.

"Years ago, when we were stationed in Germany, I decided to challenge myself to cut, piece and quilt a whole quilt in two weeks, using only fabric from my 'rag bag' which was filled with scraps that

"LIKE LOTS OF OTHER WOMEN, I QUILT TO FIND A QUIET SPACE. IT'S A FORM OF MEDITATION FOR ME. IT CENTERS ME AND HELPS ME GET IN TOUCH WITH THE DEEPEST PART OF MYSELF."

Years later she would need that faith and that strength.

In 1996, when she was 50 years old, Jerry was diagnosed with a rare form of stomach cancer.

"That's when I learned what's important in life," Jerry says. "It really boils down to just a few things. For me it's God. It's Jack and my two daughters. It's family and friends. And quilting. That's it."

Fortunately, Jerry received excellent and aggressive treatment and today her cancer is in remission. "It was rough going for awhile," she admits.

Quarters. Every time I open the door to the shop I am greeted with smiling welcoming faces," says Rita. "One of Jerry's employees recently went on vacation for a week. When she came back to work, she walked in and said 'I'm home.' That's pretty special. It's more than a store."

Jerry says that quilting has been an integral part of her recovery. She points out that many women with cancer have found quilting to be therapeutic. "My story isn't all that unique," she says. "I have lots of customers who have quilted their way through their own chemo or radiation therapy."

really were too small to be used. The quilt was to be a wall hanging, long, narrow, and vertical. As I finished the body of the quilt, I noticed that the top block was off by an 1/8 of an inch. Thinking to myself, that it would not matter much, I continued on. Well, that 1/8-inch really didn't matter until I added two borders to the quilt. Now I have a long skinny quilt that tilts its head. The finished quilt is a constant reminder to me that the little things do matter."

"A GOOD QUILT SHOPS SERVES THE SAME FUNCTION IN A WOMAN'S LIFE AS A FRONT PORCH, A BACK FENCE, OR A CORNER COFFEE SHOP."

The Quilter's Quarters
LEAVENWORTH, KS

ONE OF THE THINGS JERRY LIKES MOST ABOUT THE SHOP IS HER RELATIONSHIP WITH HER EMPLOYEES. "THESE ARE MY SISTERS," SHE SAYS OF THE WOMEN WHO WORK AND VOLUNTEER AT THE QUILTER'S QUARTERS.

THE STAFF OF THE QUILTER'S QUARTERS. CLOCKWISE FROM BOTTOM: BONNIE INGRAM, JERRY STUBE, BECKY NEAL, NANCY DIETZ, KARI LANE, RUTH LOFGREN, SUZANNE PARSONS. NOT PICTURED, JENISE CANTLON AND CINDY OLIVER.

LEAVENWORTH, KS

Make a Day of it

Located northwest of downtown Kansas City, on a bend of the Missouri River, Leavenworth is steeped in history. Fort Leavenworth was established in 1827 and, in 1854, Leavenworth became the first city in Kansas.

Leavenworth celebrates its diversity. The town helped launch thousands of covered wagons to open the West. Native American tribes, Jewish merchants, Army soldiers, including the African-American Buffalo Soldiers, Catholic nuns and state and federal prisoners called the area home.

For more information, visit the Web site of the Leavenworth Convention and Visitors Bureau, www.lvarea.com/chamber/cvb or call (800) 844-4114. Another Web site is www.lvks.org. It is always best to call ahead to check hours and days of operation for any destination.

WHAT TO SEE AND DO

Fort Leavenworth is the oldest Army fort in continuous operation west of the Mississippi River and features the oldest residence in Kansas, the Rookery. Contact the Leavenworth Convention and Visitors Bureau at (800) 844-4114 or lvcvb@lvnworth.com for a Visitors Guide with a map and self-guided tour. The fort tour includes points of interest and facts about the Oregon and Santa Fe Trails, Lewis and Clark, and Nez Perce Indians, as well as sites including the Frontier Army Museum, the National Cemetery, the Berlin Wall Monument and the Buffalo Soldiers Monument.

Fort Leavenworth is located at the north end of Leavenworth. From the Highway 92 bridge, continue west (this street becomes Metropolitan Ave.) to 7th Street, then turn north (right) to enter the main gate. Admission is free. Contact Fort Leavenworth Tourist Information at (913) 684-5604 or www.leav.army.mil/dca.

Carroll Mansion is on the National Register of Historic Places and home of the Leavenworth County Historical Society. This 1867 Victorian mansion features exquisite wood carvings, as well as furniture and antiques of the period.

Carroll Mansion is located at 1128 Fifth Avenue. From The Quilter's Quarters, go one block south, then west (left) to 4th Street Trafficway, and south (left) to Spruce. Turn west (right) on Spruce to Fifth Avenue (third light), then turn south (left) and drive three blocks. Contact (913) 682-7759 or www.leavenworth-net.com/lchs. Admission charged.

Exhibits and collections in the Richard Allen Cultural Center foster an awareness of African-American heritage, both in Leavenworth and nationwide. Richard Allen was the founder and first bishop of the African Methodist Episcopal (A.M.E.) Church

Richard Allen Cultural Center is located at 412 Kiowa. From The Quilter's Quarters, go one block north, then west (right) to 4th Street Trafficway, and north (right) to Kiowa. Turn west (left) and parking is on the northwest corner. Contact (913) 682-8772 or 682-8454. Admission charged.

THE QUILTER'S QUARTERS
219 DELAWARE STREET
LEAVENWORTH, KANSAS 66048
(913) 651-6510

Local Flavor

High Noon Saloon & Brewery is located in the grand old Great Western Building (c. 1870) on the historic riverfront warehouse district. The High Noon Saloon specializes in steaks, fajitas, barbecue and brewed on-site beer.

206 Choctow, one block south of the Quilter's Quarters, and then turn west, (913) 682-4876.

Harbor Lights Coffeehouse is not only a recommended sandwich shop, it is also the place to find creativity in caffeine — espresso, cappuccino and coffee.

303 Delaware, one block west (left) of The Quilter's Quarters, (913) 682-2303, e-mail: cafe@smartnet.net.

The Historic Skyview Restaurant, located in one of the many mansions in Leavenworth, is noted for its Victorian elegance and American cuisine. Reservations are accepted.

504 Grand, from The Quilter's Quarters, go one block south, then west (right) to 4th Street Trafficway, and south (left) to Spruce. Turn west (right) on Spruce, go through the traffic light at 10th Avenue, then turn north (right) on the next street, Grand. Drive three blocks. (913) 682-2653, www.skyviewrestaurant.net.

Make a night of it

Hallmark Inn is located on the south side of Leavenworth, near St. Mary College and the Veterans Administration Hospital, 3211 S. 4th Street Trafficway (Highway 73 and K-7). Call (888) 540-4020 for reservations.

Prairie Queen Bed & Breakfast is a restored home built in 1868, located at 221 Arch St.

From The Quilter's Quarters, go one block south, then west (left) to 4th Street Trafficway, and south (left) past Spruce to the next light at Arch. Turn east (left) on Arch, then drive two blocks. For reservations, contact (913) 758-1959 or www.prairiequeen.com.

Campsites at available at Riverfront Park. *From the Highway 92 bridge, turn south (left turn lane), drive two blocks to Dakota, turn east (left), go three blocks, cross the railroad tracks, then turn north (left) and cross under the Highway 92 bridge, (913) 682-6398.*

—Lori Wilson

Annual Events
LEAVENWORTH

In February, Hidden Art Locked Away, (913) 682-4459

In March, St. Patrick's Day Parade, (913) 682-9800

In April, Fort Leavenworth Homes Tour Frontier Army Encampment, (913) 684-5604, Ext. 5; Great American Yard Sale, (913) 684-5604, Ext. 5

In May, Annual Herb Market, (913) 682-7759

In August, Leavenworth County Fair, (913) 684-0475; Great American Yard Sale, (913) 684-5604, Ext. 5

In September, River Fest, (913) 682-3924 (Includes Quilt Show and Miniature Quilt Sale)

In October, Fort Leavenworth Antique Show, (913) 682-3509; Haunted Houses of Fort Leavenworth (913) 684-5604, Ext. 5

In November, Festival of Trees, (913) 682-5666; Veteran's Day Parade, (913) 727-3271; Annual Arts and Crafts Show, (913) 684-5604, Ext. 5

In December, Candlelight Vintage Homes Tour, (913) 682-7759

ARROWHEAD
PUBLISHED ON SEPTEMBER 27, 1937

In *The Kansas City Star* that day:

More than a million cheering people lined the streets of Berlin to greet Adolf Hitler and Benito Mussolini.

Three polio victims were released from Kansas City hospitals. No new cases of the disease were reported during the preceding weekend.

The federal government files suit against gangster Al Capone for back income taxes in the amount of $270,011.96.

A Japanese submarine attacks and sinks a fleet of Chinese fishing boats killing over 300 men, women and children.

Block sizes: 6", 8", 12" and 24"

FOR EACH BLOCK, CUT:

6" Block

A Sixteen 1 1/4" squares of dark fabric and twenty-four 1 1/4" squares of light or background fabric.

B Four 3/4" strips of light or background fabric.

C Four 3/4" strips of light or background fabric.

D Four 1 5/8" squares (cut in half diagonally) of light or background fabric.

E Four 2 3/4" squares (cut in half diagonally twice) of medium fabric and 1 of light or background fabric.

F One 2" square of light or background fabric.

8" Block

A Sixteen 1 1/2" squares of dark fabric and twenty-four 1 1/2" squares of light or background fabric.

B Four 7/8" strips of light or background fabric.

C Four 7/8" strips of light or background fabric.

D Four 1 7/8" squares (cut in half diagonally) of light or background fabric.

E Four 3 1/4" squares (cut in half diagonally twice) of medium fabric and 1 of light or background fabric.

F One 2 1/2" square of light or background fabric.

12" Block

A Sixteen 2" squares of dark fabric and twenty-four 2" squares of light or background fabric.

B Four 1 1/8" strips of light or background fabric.

C Four 1 1/8" strips of light or background fabric.

D Four 2 3/8" squares (cut in half diagonally) of light or background fabric.

E Four 4 1/4" squares (cut in half diagonally twice) of medium fabric and 1of light or background fabric.

F One 3 1/2" square of light or background fabric.

24" Block

A Sixteen 3 1/2" squares of dark fabric and twenty-four 3 1/2" squares of light or background fabric.

B Four 1 3/4" strips of light or background fabric.

C Four 1 3/4" strips of light or background fabric.

D Four 3 7/8" squares (cut in half diagonally) of light or background fabric.

E Four 7 1/4" squares (cut in half diagonally twice) of medium fabric and 1 of light or background fabric.

F One 6 1/2" square of light or background fabric.

"KANSAS CITY LITTLE DUDES"
PIECED AND QUILTED BY SUZANNE PARSONS.

SEE OTHER QUILTS BASED ON THIS PATTERN ON PAGES 74-77.

For each corner of the block, assemble a nine-patch unit in the size selected with the dark "A" block positioned as shown and set these aside.

Using a dark "A" square, sew a "B" strip to one side. Add a "C" strip to the opposing side of the square as shown.

Cut the "D" pieces according to the size chosen. Add one piece to each side of the square as shown.

Sew a medium "E" piece to one side of the unit as shown.

Sew a medium "E" piece to a light "E" piece and add it to the unit. This will complete the center unit. Make three more of these units.

To assemble the block, sew a nine-patch unit to opposing sides of a center unit as shown. Make another row like this.

For the middle row, sew a center unit to opposing sides of an "F" square that will look like this.

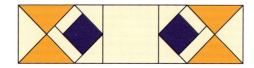

Sew the three rows together to complete the block.

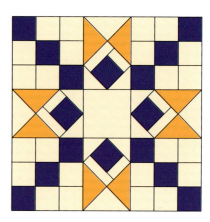

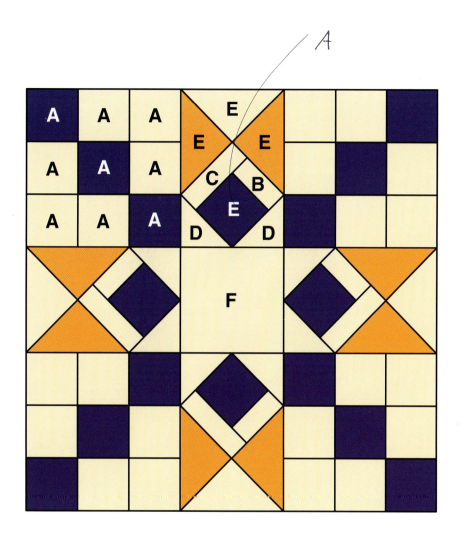

_A_

Quilter's Station
LEE'S SUMMIT, MISSOURI

Rita Briner is The All-American Girl all grown up.

She was raised on a farm near Polo, Missouri, north of Kansas City, and like other farm kids she was active in 4-H and was something of a tomboy. Like most farm wives, Rita's mother was a skilled seamstress and she tried to teach her daughter how to sew. "All my mom's friend's daughters were making their own doll clothes," Rita says. "But I always had a football or baseball in my hand, never a needle."

Pretty, and popular in school, Rita was a cheerleader, she played flute in the band and sang in the choir. And eventually she did learn to sew.

"The summer between 6th and 7th grade I made all my school clothes for the next year," she recalls. "And then when I was in high school I sewed for the other girls to

earn spending money. I was pretty industrious. I also mowed yards and cleaned houses."

Industrious is an understatement. Rita graduated second in her high school class.

The most significant event in Rita's life occurred when she was eight years old. That's when she went to live with her grandfather, Smith Webb. Smith was also a farmer and Rita helped him with his livestock and with housework.

"It was just a magic time for me," Rita recalls. "I felt like I was in a storybook."

Rita lived with her grandfather until he died. She was ten years old.

"I really believe he's been with me my whole life," Rita says. "He's my guardian angel. He watches over everything I do and helps me."

QUILTER'S STATION
824 SW BLUE PARKWAY
LEE'S SUMMIT, MISSOURI 64063
(816) 525-8955
WEB ADDRESS: WWW.QUILTERSSTATION.COM
E-MAIL: QUILTERSSTATION@PRODIGY.COM
ESTABLISHED IN 1995
OVER 3,500 BOLTS OF FABRIC
5 EMPLOYEES

LEE'S SUMMIT

YOU
CAN HELP
QUILT
FOR A CURE
CURE
BREAST
CANCER

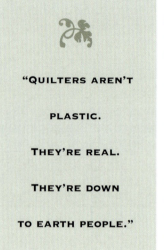

"BEING A QUILT SHOP OWNER IS A LOT LIKE BEING A BARTENDER. YOU HAVE TO BE A GOOD LISTENER, BECAUSE CUSTOMERS WILL COME IN AND TELL YOU EVERY PROBLEM THEY HAVE EVER HAD. BUT THAT'S ONE OF THE GOOD THINGS ABOUT A QUILT SHOP. YOU MAKE CONNECTIONS."

It's easy to conclude that Rita has benefited from heavenly intervention. She's the owner and operator of Quilter's Station in Lee's Summit, Missouri. She's been in business since 1995. A year later the store was enjoying such success that she moved the business to a larger space. In 1998, she had to expand into the space next door to accommodate the shop's growth. And then in 2001 the store was expanded yet again.

Rita made her first quilts when her children were born. "They were just small baby quilts," she says. "Actually, it didn't even occur to me at the time that I was quilting. It was just something I wanted to do for my babies."

It was later that the quilting bug bit her, and bit her hard. It was during a visit to a museum gift shop in Lancaster, Pennsylvania. There she saw a quilt for sale for $450. *I can do that,* she thought, mentally calculating the cost and profit of such an effort. And when she got home, that's what she did.

The quilt she made was the "Tree of Life" appliques quilt with more than 1,000 pieces. "I suppose I could have picked an easier one to start with," she admits, laughing. "But it got me hooked. I've been quilting ever since."

Rita made quilts for five years before she enrolled in her first quilt class. Now, one of the things she likes most about owning a quilt shop is helping beginners, like she once was.

Linda Brannock, a Kansas City fabric designer, has observed Rita's interactions with her customers. "She really makes every effort to learn about them and to help meet their individual needs," she says. "She's cultivated a very loyal following. She's admired for the quality of her work, which is meticulous and beautiful, but she's also admired for the quality of her friendship."

Brannock admits that another reason she likes hanging out at Quilter's Station is that Rita serves great snacks.

Klonda Holt, a schoolbus driver and loyal customer, says that Rita's quilts are an inspiration. "Her work is great," she states. "We all wish we could create quilts as beautiful as Rita's. But it's really her kindness that keeps us all coming back. That, and the dog."

Klonda is referring to Licorice, the energetic and friendly little black dog that greets all Quilter's Station customers.

For Rita a quilt shop is more than just a business. It's a place for women to connect with one another and to form lasting friendships and support networks.

Rita observes that quilting is a lot like running. "You can get into a rhythm, almost a trance-like state," she says. "It releases you from your cares and frustrations."

Pushing the metaphor even further she says "Sometimes, when you really need a good work out you have to run by yourself. But it's always a lot more fun to go out for a run with friends. A quilt shop is the best place to meet people to 'run' with. "

"QUILTERS AREN'T PLASTIC. THEY'RE REAL. THEY'RE DOWN TO EARTH PEOPLE."

Quilter's Station
LEE'S SUMMIT, MO

**THE QUILTER'S STATION STAFF. LEFT TO RIGHT;
SHIRLEY DUNCAN, RITA BRINER, PAT SHACKELFORD.**

Lee's Summit began as part of the 2,300 acres owned by William B. Howard in the mid 1800s. Location, as Howard discovered, is the key in real estate. The railroads were moving west and the landowner secured the right of way by striking a deal with the Pacific Railroad.

Rail travel is still important, with an Amtrak station near the Historic Lee's Summit Train Depot in the heart of downtown. The depot serves as the home of Lee's Summit Museum (tours by appointment), Chamber of Commerce and the Economic Development Council.

For more information, contact (888) 647-6280 or www.lstourism.com.

It is always best to call ahead to check hours and days of operation for any destination.

What to see and do

Powell Gardens is 20 miles east of Lee's Summit. This 915-acre botanical garden is filled with thousands of colorful plants, pathways and meadows. It is also the only place in the world with three structures designed by architect Fay Jones.

1609 N. W. Highway 50, Kingsville, Mo., from Quilters Station, take Highway 50 east approximately 20 miles, continue east through Lone Jack and watch for the Powell Gardens signs. Turn north (left) from the left lane. Admission charged, (816) 697-2600, www.powellgardens.org.

Unity Village is the world headquarters of the Unity School of Christianity, a religious and educational institution founded in 1889.

The Mediterranean-style structures of Unity Village are listed on the National Register of Historic Places.

1901 N.W. Blue Parkway, from Quilters Station, take Highway 50 west to the Unity Village exit. Free tours, (816) 251-3565 or www.unityworld-hq.org.

Located 10 minutes east of Lee's Summit is a tribute to The Battle of Lone Jack, one of the bloodiest Civil War battles in Missouri. The battlefield site includes a museum, with tours available by appointment, as well as a cemetery.

301 S. Bynum, Lone Jack, Mo., from Quilters Station, take Highway 50 east approximately 10 miles to Lone Jack, then take the Bynum Road exit south to the Lone Jack Battlefield, Museum and Cemetery, admission charged, (816) 566-2272 or Lone Jack City Hall at (816) 697-2503.

Local flavor

The Filling Station (pictured left) is a successful competitor in a barbecue town. Kids' favorites are also on the menu. All ages will eat up the nostalgia of its location - a restored Texaco station built in the early 1900s.

333 S. E. Douglas, from Quilters Station, turn right (northwest) to Third, take Third east to the downtown area, turn south (right) at Douglas. The Filling Station is at the corner of Fourth and Douglas, (816) 347-0794.

Neighbor's Café is the home of home cooking, where you'll find your meat-and-potatoes favorites, and breakfast fare such as their popular biscuits and gravy. Everyone gets a free homemade cinnamon roll.

104 East Third, from Quilters Station, turn right (northwest) to Third, take Third east to the downtown area, past the light at Douglas. Neighbor's Café is on the northeast corner, (816) 524-1069.

Tuscany Manor highlights fine dining favorites of seafood, Angus steaks and pasta in a 1902 restored home.

300 Missouri Road, from Quilters Station, drive Highway 50 west to I-470 east, then exit at Douglas, drive south and Tuscany Manor is on the southeast corner, behind Hampton Inn, (816) 246-8588.

MAKE A NIGHT OF IT

Summit Inn and Suites, locally owned and operated, features a continental breakfast, restaurant, outdoor pool and fitness center.

Details: 625 N. W. Murray Road, from Quilters Station, drive north on Highway 50, exit on Chipman Road, drive west (left) , go under 50 Highway and, at the second light, turn south (left), (816) 525-1400 or (800) 528-1234.

At Holiday Inn Express, near I-70, you can enjoy an indoor pool, hot tub, fitness room and continental breakfast with your stay.

4825 N. E. Lakewood Way, from Quilters Station, drive Highway 50 west. After it curves to the north, exit at I-470 east to Highway 291 north, exit at Bowlin Road, turn east (right), then take the first south turn (right), (816) 795-6400, (800) HOLIDAY, www.sixcontinentshotels.com/hiexpress?_franchisee=MKCLS

Camping is available through Jackson County Parks and Recreation at two locations: Longview Lake and Blue Springs Lake.

Details: (816) 229-8980

—Lori Wilson

Annual Events
LEE'S SUMMIT

In May, beach season opens at Longview Lake, (816) 795-8200 Ext. 1-276

In June, Old Tyme Days, (816) 246-6598

July, Christmas in July Craft Sale, (816) 246-4343, Ext. 4235

In August, Festival of Butterflies at Powell Gardens, (816) 697-2600

In September, Mini Golf Classic, (816) 524-2424

In October, Halloween Parade, (816) 246-6598

In November and December, Christmas in the Park, (816) 795-8200, Ext. 1-225

QUILTER'S STATION
824 SW BLUE PARKWAY
LEE'S SUMMIT, MISSOURI 64063
(816) 525-8955

ABOVE : THE MARJORIE POWELL
ALLEN CHAPEL AT POWELL GARDENS

TWENTIETH CENTURY STAR

PUBLISHED ON APRIL 6, 1938

In *The Kansas City Star* that day:

Pope Pius demands that Adolf Hitler guarantee the rights of Catholics in Austria.

Dr. Sigmund Freud, under threat of arrest by Nazi occupiers, announces plans to leave Austria for England.

While visiting the Welsh National museum, Britain's Queen Mother sadly views an exhibit of items once belonging to her son, the Duke of Windsor, the former King Edward VIII.

In Hollywood, comedian Jack Benny reports that his limousine is stolen.

Block Size: 12"
Quilt Size: 82 x 82

Fabric needed: 4 yards of navy blue, 3 yards of red and 1 1/2 yards of gold. You will need 6 1/2 yards for the backing.

Cut out the pieces for each block using the templates given. Sew an F, G, H, J and I piece to each star. To add these pieces, start sewing at each point of the star and sew toward the center. Continue until all the units are in place as shown.

Press each seam away from the star.

Sew the A piece to the B piece and the C piece to the D piece. Sew these two units together forming a circle. Fold the star unit in fourths and finger press the creases. Match the creases to the four seams of the circle. Pin the star unit to the circular outer unit and sew to complete the block as shown.

To make the setting blocks (or alternate blocks), cut twelve 12 1/2" squares from the navy fabric and cut forty-eight 4 1/2" squares using the red fabric. Draw a diagonal line on each of the 4 1/2" red squares. Place one red square on each corner of a navy square and sew on the line. Trim the seam 1/4" from the stitched line and press.

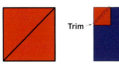

After all the blocks are constructed, join the blocks together in rows. There are five blocks to a row and five rows make up the center of the quilt.

Each row is made alternating a star block with a setting block. Row one begins and ends with a star block. The second row will begin and end with a setting block. Continue in this manner until the rows are complete. Sew the rows together to complete the center.

Measure the center of the quilt across the top, the bottom and the center. Taking the smallest measurement, cut the inner border 2 1/2" by this measurement and add 3" on each end. This will enable you to miter the corners. Sew these strips to the center of the quilt.

Cut two 4 1/2" navy squares and two 4 1/2" red squares. Set these aside. Cut thirty-two 4 7/8" navy squares and thirty-two 4 7/8" red squares. Mark a diagonal line on the back of each red square. Place a red square on top of each blue square with right sides facing. Sew 1/4" on each side of the line. Cut along the line and press the half-square triangles open. Sew 8 of these units together keeping the navy to the outside as shown.

Turn the next 8 units and sew them together keeping the navy to the outside. Join this strip to the first strip. Two red squares will touch each other in the center as shown.

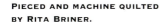

Make four of these strips. Sew a strip to two sides of the quilt. Sew a red square to each end of one of the remaining strips. Sew a navy square to each end of the other strip. Add these to the top and bottom of the quilt.

For the last quilt border, cut six 6 1/2" x 42" strips of red and six 6 1/2" x 42" strips of navy. Make a side border by sewing three navy strips together. You will need two of these strips. Sew three strips of red together to make another side border. Again, you will need two strips like this. Measure the quilt top again across the top, middle and bottom. Make sure your strips are 6 1/2" longer than the quilt for mitering purposes. Add these borders to the quilt by placing the red strips on one of the sides and the top of the quilt. Add the two navy borders to the other two sides to complete the quilt.

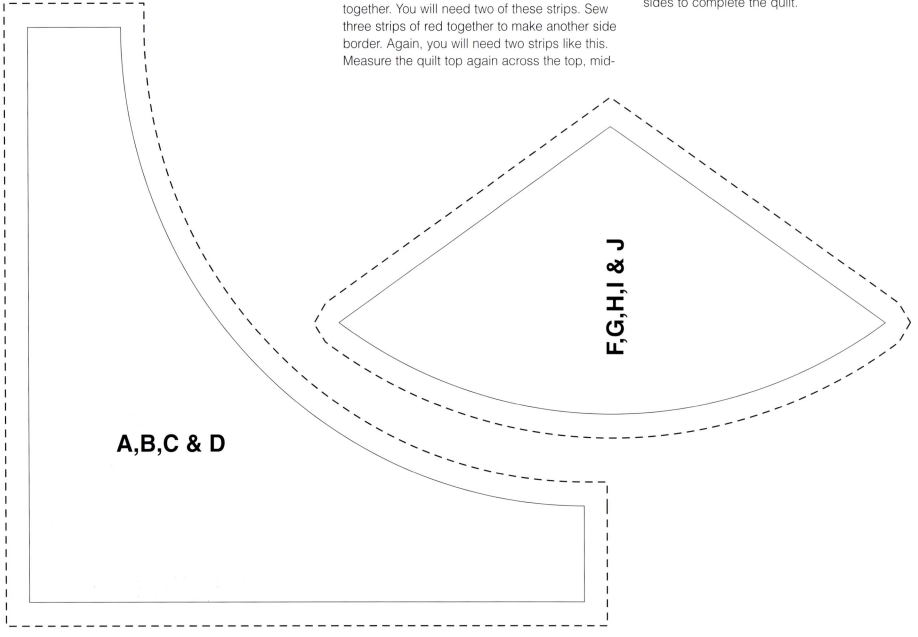

F,G,H,I & J

A,B,C & D

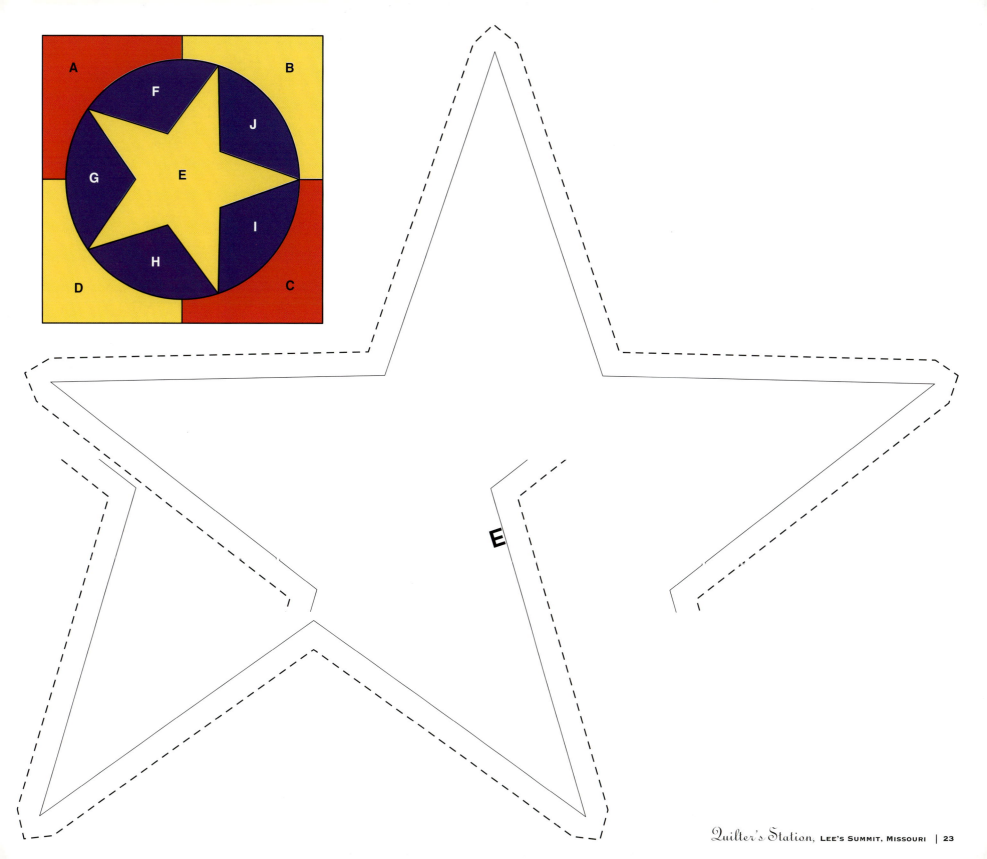

E

Kansas City
A Quilting Capital

*T*he Kansas/Missouri region of the United States is to quilting what the Bordeaux region of France is to wine. It's the place where the craft is practiced at its peak. It's where the best of the best comes from.

For generations the vintners of Bordeaux have toiled in the sun, pruning their vines, harvesting and pressing their grapes, patiently waiting for time to work its way, and then, when the time is right, bottling it. The fortunate few who drink the resulting wine are tasting the perfection of the vintner's craft.

Likewise, for generations the women of America's heartland have, in church basements, spare bedrooms, and store-front backrooms, bent over their fabric, cutting, piecing, and stitching to create quilts of surpassing beauty and

ingenuity. Those whose beds or walls are graced with these quilts are blessed with the finest examples of a time-honored tradition, preserved and advanced by tireless women of dedication and imagination.

While a church basement in Kansas is not nearly so idyllic a setting as a hillside vineyard in France, it is, as it turns out, just as important in perpetuating a cherished cultural custom.

Barbara Brackman, one of America's premier quilt historians, says that as interest in quilting faded among many American women in the mid-20th century, it was rural churchwomen who kept the craft alive.

"Specifically, Methodist women," states Brackman. "It seems that quilting bees were the favored fundraising techniques among Methodist women. If a church needed

LEFT: RUBY SHORT MCKIM AND HER DAUGHTERS. MCKIN DESIGNED THE FIRST KANSAS CITY STAR QUILT PATTERN IN 1928.

QUILTERS IN MEADE COUNTY, KANSAS EARLY TWENTIETH CENTURY.

KANSAS CITY STAR FASHION/QUILT EDITOR EDNA MARIE DUNN. DUNN HELPED SELECT MANY OF THE CLASSIC STAR PATTERNS.

BARBARA BRACKMAN, QUILT HISTORIAN

KANSAS CITY

money for missions, Sunday school materials, or for a new addition to its church building, the women of the congregation made quilts together that they would then sell, or auction, or raffle. I believe that one of the primary reasons the Midwest is such a hotbed of quilting activity today is because the highest concentration of Methodists is in the state of Iowa. And the second highest number is in Kansas. Quilting was

selling just the patterns themselves and those sold quite well."

The patterns provided women with the means of making quilts using their own fabric from a variety of sources; from old clothes to flour sacks.

In those days, it was a common practice for Midwestern newspapers to regularly feature quilt patterns, sometimes as frequently as once a

That's one of the primary reasons our quilt patterns became so widely known."

The legendary *Kansas City Star* quilt patterns are, in fact, another major factor contributing to the long term vitality of quilting in the Midwest in general and in the Kansas and Missouri specifically.

Ruby McKim, who lived in Independence,

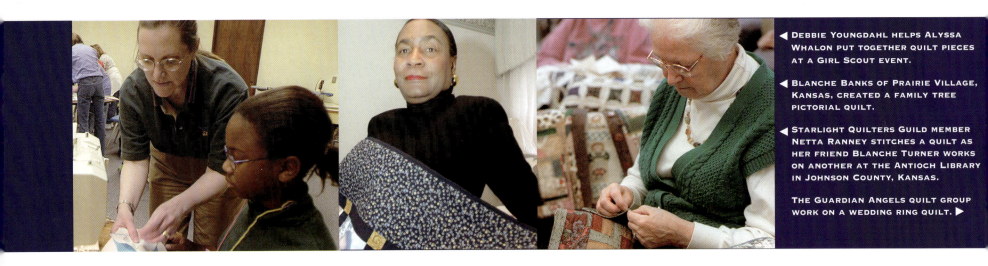

◀ DEBBIE YOUNGDAHL HELPS ALYSSA WHALON PUT TOGETHER QUILT PIECES AT A GIRL SCOUT EVENT.

◀ BLANCHE BANKS OF PRAIRIE VILLAGE, KANSAS, CREATED A FAMILY TREE PICTORIAL QUILT.

◀ STARLIGHT QUILTERS GUILD MEMBER NETTA RANNEY STITCHES A QUILT AS HER FRIEND BLANCHE TURNER WORKS ON ANOTHER AT THE ANTIOCH LIBRARY IN JOHNSON COUNTY, KANSAS.

THE GUARDIAN ANGELS QUILT GROUP WORK ON A WEDDING RING QUILT. ▶

an activity in other denominations as well, but in my research I found that it was most popular among Methodists."

Brackman explains that there were other factors as well that helped keep quilting viable. During the Depression, quilting was a way for individual rural women to make money. But not, as it turns out, by making and selling quilts themselves.

"Apparently, few people could afford completed quilts," Brackman says. "So women tried selling quilt kits made up of the pieces and the instructions. Those didn't sell either. So women tried

week. Certainly the primary reason for this was a desire on the part of the newspapers to cultivate their rural readerships. Another motivation may have been to fill space in the newspapers' pages as advertising decreased during tough economic times.

The Kansas City Star was one of the first to provide patterns to its readers. The current editor of *The Star,* Mark Zieman, explains that back then the newspaper had a much broader geographic distribution than it does today. "*The Star* was read by folks from Nebraska to Oklahoma. We were as much a rural paper as a city paper.

Missouri, designed the first *Star* quilt pattern which was published on September 22, 1928. McKim, who was also needlework editor for *Better Homes and Gardens* magazine, is considered to be among the most important 20th century quilt designers. Her patterns have remained popular for nearly eight decades.

The Kansas City area was also home to other major quilt designers, including Rose Kretsinger of Emporia, Kansas. Kretsinger, who earned a degree from the Art Institute of Chicago, created quilts of such sophisticated creativity that she was the subject of a (unprecedented at the time)

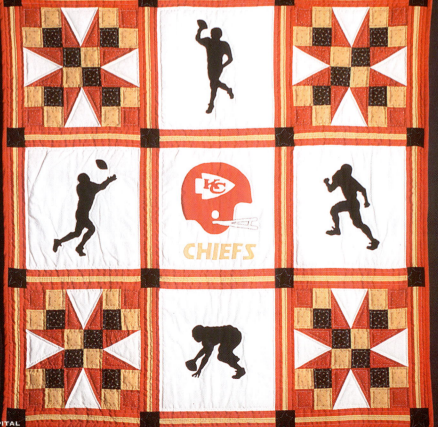

NEIGHBORHOOD WOMEN GATHER AT THE RED BRIDGE LIBRARY IN KANSAS CITY TO LEARN QUILTING.

THE KANSAS CITY CHIEFS PRO FOOTBALL TEAM IS THE THEME OF THIS QUILT.

one-woman show staged by the Kansas City Art Institute.

During the 1930s, a number of extraordinarily gifted quilter lived in Emporia, including Charlotte Jane Whitehill, Josephine Craig, and Hannah Haynes Headlee. Scioto Imhoff Danner, another quilt master from the same era, lived in El Dorado, Kansas.

These days, the Kansas City area is headquarters to quilting royalty Chris Wolf Edmonds, Terry Thompson and the aforementioned Barbara Brackman. Brackman, however, is quick to point out that she is not herself a quilt maker. "I love quilts. I have lots of quilts. But what I am is a historian. My contribution to quilting has been to raise the standards for looking at the history of the craft."

Brackman has also contributed several important books to the quilting literature, the latest of which is *Prairie Flower, A Year On The Plains: New Applique Patterns in The Kansas City Star tradition.*

"Who knows why the Kansas City area has been blessed with so many great quilt designers over the years," Brackman asks. "I've told people that there must be something in the water here. And I'm really hard pressed to explain how or why Emporia, Kansas, was such a quilting capital there for a while. But whatever the reason, we've been enriched by the lives of these innovative artists who were willing to teach and share their talent with others."

In Brackman's research she has discovered no distinctive "Kansas Style" or "Missouri Style" quilt. "This area isn't known for a particular style," she explains. "Rather it's known for exceptional quality, creativity, and integrity of craftsmanship."

In Kansas City today quilting is used as an educational tool in area schools. It is taught in college curricula. It is a respected art form and the subject of exhibits and shows. It is as vital and alive as ever.

The reasons why quilting is popular today are the same as they've always been: it is a creative means of expressing oneself. And while quilting

a quilt that makes it both practical yet loaded with emotional connotation and memory."

As Americans have become increasingly emotionally and culturally isolated in economically and ethnically segregated suburbs, quilting, it seems, is one way of creating community.

In quilt shops, church basements and community centers throughout the country, and especially

"Quilts give us a sense of shared history. I'm from New York City," she points out. "I come from a family of Jewish Russian immigrants. Frankly, quilting is not a part of my personal heritage. But I am an American woman. And I feel a kinship to American women who have come before me. And quilting was a part of their lives. And quilts connect me to them, regardless of my personal ancestry."

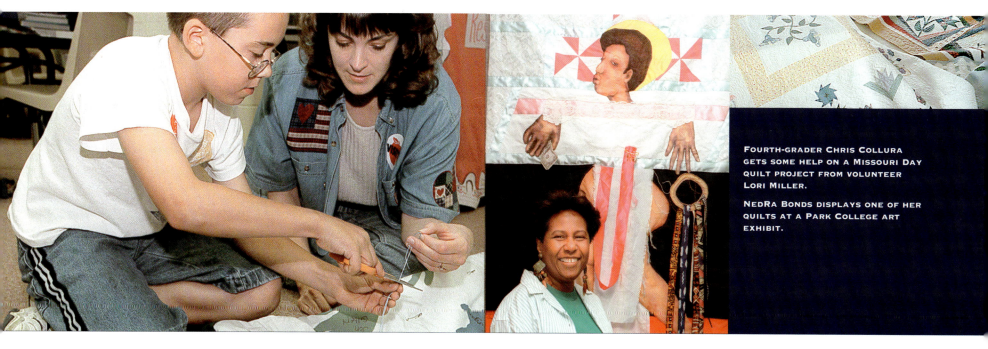

FOURTH-GRADER CHRIS COLLURA GETS SOME HELP ON A MISSOURI DAY QUILT PROJECT FROM VOLUNTEER LORI MILLER.

NEDRA BONDS DISPLAYS ONE OF HER QUILTS AT A PARK COLLEGE ART EXHIBIT.

requires skill and effort, the skills and efforts required seem to the novice accessible and achievable. And, as hobbies go, it is relatively affordable.

Quilting fits relatively easily in most women's lifestyles. It is an activity that can be picked up and put down whenever convenient or necessary.

"People respect the final product," Brackman says. "There is a functionality and an intimacy to

here in the Kansas City area, women are forming communities around quilting. These communities extend support to their members in every way a community should, sharing the joys and burdens of ordinary life.

Quilting is far more an expression of community than a means of making blankets. "There's lots easier ways to get warm than to cut up fabric and put it back together," Brackman concedes with a laugh.

You may want to make that two days. Or a week. Or just come back again and again to take in all Kansas City has to offer.

The famous Midwestern hospitality of Kansas City has drawn small town folks, big city slickers and people in between from around the world and around the bend.

Some visitors expect a heaping helping of country music and get sides of jazz, blues, modern rock and The Kansas City Symphony.

When it's time to eat, "American" food means a melting pot of ethnic flavors — Italian, Irish, Greek, Vietnamese, Indian, Mediterranean, Mexican, Spanish, French, and Cajun. And, of course, there's always plenty of burgers and steaks in Kansas City.

Many tourists come for the legendary barbecue, then are surprised with a summer taste of the arts such as Shakespeare in the Park.

Every sports fan knows the Chiefs and Royals, but other pros play in Kansas City too - the Attack play soccer indoors and the Wizards get their kicks outside. The Knights shoot hoops on the basketball court during winter and spring months and, in the summer, the Explorers serve up tennis. Auto racing fans can make tracks to the new local venue - Kansas Speedway.

Even if Midwestern hospitality wasn't invented here, Kansas City carries on the tradition with affordable fun, friendliness and variety.

There's so much to see and do it'll be difficult for you to decide how to spend your time in Kansas City. Here are just a few things choose from:

American Jazz Museum, 1616 East 18th, Kansas City, Mo., (816) 474-8463, www.americanjazzmuseum.com

Arabia Steamboat Museum, 400 Grand Blvd, Kansas City, Mo., (816) 471-4030, www.1856.com

Bingham-Waggoner Estate, 313 W. Pacific, Independence, Mo., (816) 461-3491, www.bwestate.org

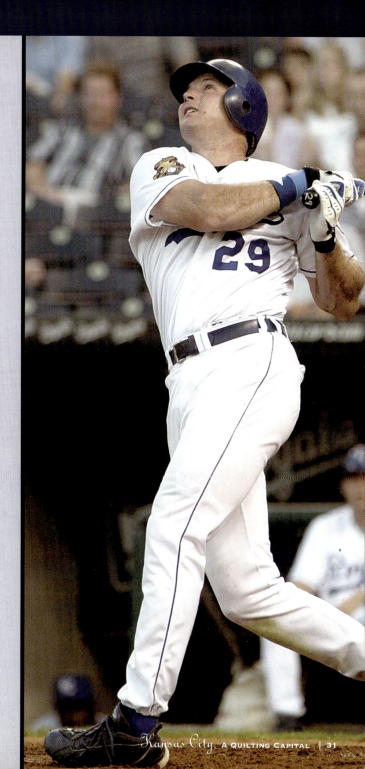

Grinter Place State Historic Site, 1420 S. 78th (Hwy. 32), Kansas City, Kan., (913) 299-0373, www.kshs.org/places/grinter.htm

Kansas City Chiefs, One Arrowhead Drive, Kansas City, Mo., (816) 920-9400, www.kcchiefs.com

Kansas City Royals, Kauffman Stadium, (800) 676-9257, www.kcroyals.com

Kansas City Zoo, Swope Park, Kansas City, Mo., (816) 513-5701, www.kansascityzoo.org

Kansas Speedway, 400 Speedway Blvd., Kansas City, Kan., (913) 328-3300, www.kansasspeedway.com

Missouri Town 1855, Lake Jacomo, Fleming Park, Blue Springs, Mo., (816) 795-8200, Ext. 1260

National Agricultural Center and Hall of Fame, 630 Hall of Fame Drive, Bonner Springs, Kan., (913) 721-1075, www.aghalloffame.com

Negro Leagues Baseball Museum, 1616 East 18th, Kansas City, Mo., (816) 221-1920, www.nlbm.com

Nelson-Atkins Museum of Art, 4525 Oak Street, Kansas City, Mo., (816) 561-4000, www.nelson-atkins.org

Science City at Union Station, 30 West Pershing Road, Kansas City, Mo., (816) 460-2020, www.sciencecity.com

Worlds of Fun and Oceans of Fun, 4545 Worlds of Fun Avenue, Kansas City, Mo., (816) 454-4545, www.worldsoffun.com

Toy and Miniature Museum, 5235 Oak, Kansas City, Mo., (816) 333-2055, www.umkc.edu/tmm

Truman Presidential Museum and Library, U. S. Highway 24 and Delaware, Independence, Mo., (800) 833-1225, www.trumanlibrary.org

Vaile Victorian Mansion, 1500 N. Liberty, Independence, Mo., (816) 325-7430, www.vailemansion.org

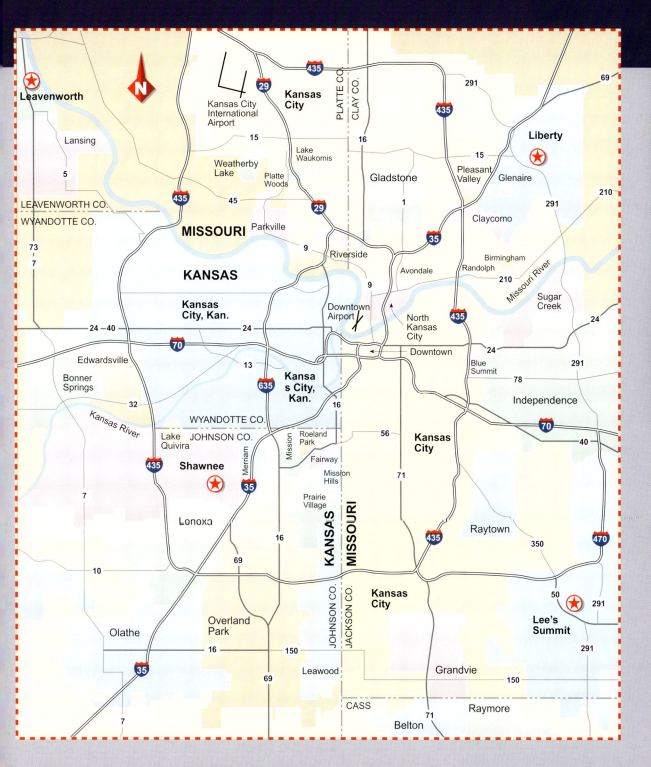

LOCAL FLAVOR

Kansas City has crowned itself king of barbecue and many around the world agree. No matter which type of cuisine your taste buds are craving, you'll probably find it in Kansas City. *Goin' to Kansas City* magazine is an excellent resource with an up-to-date restaurant listing. It is published quarterly by the Convention and Visitors Bureau of Greater Kansas City. Find them online at www.gointokansascity.com or call (800) 767-7700 to request a printed copy by mail.

Another resource is the Missouri Restaurant Association at www.morestaurant.org or (816) 753-5222.

Make a night of it

Lodging is available all over the Kansas City area, in hotels, motels and bed & breakfast inns. *Goin' to Kansas City* magazine is also an excellent resource for lodging.

Another resource is the Hotel and Motel Association of Greater Kansas City, (816) 421-3646 or www.kansascitylodging.org.

—*Lori Wilson*

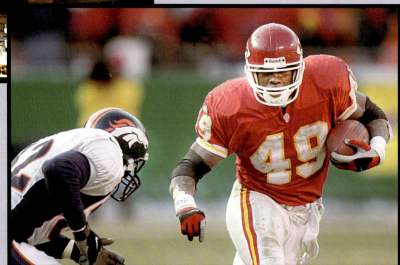

TOP LEFT: UNION STATION ON THE FOURTH OF JULY; TOP RIGHT: LIBERTY MEMORIAL; BOTTOM, RIGHT: KANSAS CITY CHIEF RUNS FOR DAYLIGHT. FAR PAGE: THE NELSON-ATKINS MUSEUM OF ART.

Annual Events
KANSAS CITY AREA

In January, Kansas City Sportshow, (816) 513-5000

In February, Kansas City RV & Outdoor Fun Show; Kansas City Boat Show; World of Wheels Show, (816) 513-5000

In March, Greater Kansas City Auto Show; Home Show, (816) 513-5000; St. Patrick's Day Parade, (816) 931-7373

In April, Greater Kansas City Quilt Shop Hop, (913) 651-6510; Spring Herb and Plant Show, (816) 444-1858

In May, Cinco de Mayo, (816) 221-4747; Brookside Art Annual, (816) 523-5553

In June, Strawberry Festival, (816) 325-7430; Settlers Day, (816) 792-2655

In July, Jaycees Pro Rodeo, (816) 761-1234; Blues and Jazz Festival, (800) 530-KCMO

In August, Aviation Expo and Airshow, (816) 221-4448; Ethnic Enrichment Festival, (816) 513-7593

On Labor Day weekend, Spirit Festival, (816) 221-4444; Santa-Cali-Gon Days, (816) 252-4745; Santa-Cali-Gon Quilt Show, (816) 257-5588; Renaissance Festival, Bonner Springs, Kan., (800) 363-0357

In September, Heart of America Quilt Festival, (816) 274-8537; Plaza Art Fair (816) 753-0100

In October, Birds of a Feather Quilt Show, (913) 851-8995; Starlight Quilter's Guild Quilt Show, (816) 523-6792; several Octoberfests throughout the city

In November, American Royal Livestock, Horse Show and Rodeo, (816) 221-7979; Country Club Plaza Season of Lights begins (816) 753-0100

In December, Kansas City is full of festivals and events for the holidays. See www.visitkc.com/visitor for more information.

Other helpful sources are www.kansascity.com, sponsored by The Kansas City Star, and www.gointokansascity.com, sponsored by the Convention and Visitors Bureau of Greater Kansas City. You may also call their 24-hour visitor information line at (800) 767-7700. It is always best to call ahead to check hours and days of operation for any destination.

Jeanne Poore
WINNING COACH

J Jeanne Poore is an evangelist, spreading the word, reaching out, teaching new converts of the joys of quilting.

Jeanne herself was converted at a young age. At age 13 Jeanne finished a quilt her paternal great-grandmother - who was born in 1858 - had started. Today, she is one of the Midwest's busiest and most respected quilting teachers and lecturers.

"Church quilting bees were just a part of my life when I was young," Jeanne says. "So I don't really remember a time when I wasn't surrounded by quilts."

Quilts are both a way of life and a livelihood for Jeanne Poore. She's a quilt pattern designer. Her business is called JePo Designs. Her finished quilts have been photographed for and featured on the covers and in the pages of national quilting magazines. Her quilts have won awards and prizes at county and state fairs and juried shows. She's been an active leader of several local and regional quilt guilds. And her classes routinely fill up with quilters of all skill levels eager to learn more from an accomplished quiltmaker.

Sally Kennedy, who has been a quilter for 25 years says the Jeanne is a gifted teacher. "She won't talk down to you or over you," she states. "She inspires her students and instills them with confidence."

Something Sally especially admires is that Jeanne herself she takes classes from other teachers. "As good as she is, she knows she can still learn. There's no arrogance in her."

Sarah Cullins agrees. Sarah is another 25-year quilter who has also taken classes from Jeanne. "She's very patient.

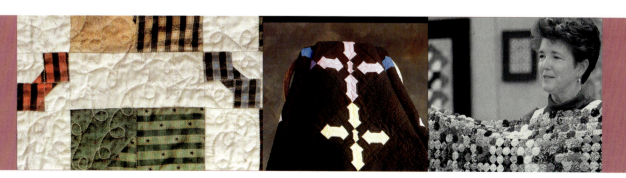

JEANNE POORE COMES FROM A LONG LINE OF LONG-LIVED WOMEN. HER GREAT GRANDMA, WHOM JEANNE CALLED LITTLE GRANDMA, LIVED TO BE 97. HER MATERNAL GRANDMOTHER LIVED TO BE 88 AND HER PATERNAL GRANDMOTHER LIVED TO THE AGE OF 89.

JEANNE AND HER HUSBAND RECENTLY CELEBRATED THEIR 40TH WEDDING ANNIVERSARY. THE TWO MET IN GRADE SCHOOL.

JEANNE HAS TWO GROWN CHILDREN, A SON AND A DAUGHTER, AND THREE "ABSOLUTELY WONDERFUL" GRANDCHILDREN.

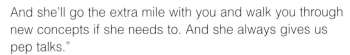

And she'll go the extra mile with you and walk you through new concepts if she needs to. And she always gives us pep talks."

That's what a coach does. Give pep talks. Give confidence.

"I guess I never used the word 'coach' to describe myself," she admits. "But I suppose it fits. I'm always trying to gently push the students in my classes to new achieve at a higher level. The first class I taught was called 'Anyone Can Quilt'. And one of my lectures is titled 'You Can Too.' So there is that theme of encouraging people try new things and to get them past their fears or inhibitions about quilting.

"The quilts pictured in the magazines and books, and the ones displayed at the shows all seem to be so elaborate perfectly made that it can intimidate a beginning quilter. In fact, they may scare some people away from even trying their first quilt. My message is this: Start with what you *can* do and build on that."

Jeanne's philosophy is that quilting should be fun or that it should satisfy something inside one's soul.

"Sometimes people quilt for reasons other than enjoyment," she points out. "There are a lot of 'cancer' quilts that women have made to help them get through cancer treatments for themselves or loved ones. And there are 'mourning' quilts

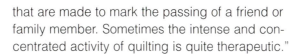

that are made to mark the passing of a friend or family member. Sometimes the intense and concentrated activity of quilting is quite therapeutic."

Because quilting is so therapeutic, she sees its popularity continuing to grow.

"Women and their families are so busy these days that the need for something restorative is greater than ever," she explains. "Plus there's so much good information about quilting out there with the Internet. And it's become very accessible."

It seems that Jeanne will have a steady supply of new students to teach for quite a while. And like a good evangelist or coach she never gets tired of sharing. And she still gets a thrill witnessing a new student discover quilting's joys.

"When one of my students brings me a picture of their finished quilt, gets an award, get their quilts pictured in books and magazines or simply say to me that they learned even one thing in the class that made it worthwhile to them, I am happy for them. And, of course, a feeling a fulfillment for me because I have helped them achieve a goal."

"QUILTS ARE AN AMERICAN TRADITION. A LEGACY THAT WOMEN HAVE SUSTAINED THROUGH THE YEARS. BUT FOR ME, QUILTING IS ALSO A HIGHLY PERSONAL CONNECTION TO BOTH THE PAST AND THE FUTURE - THROUGH THE QUILTS MY GRANDMOTHERS MADE AND THE QUILTS I HAVE MADE FOR MY CHILDREN AND GRANDCHILDREN. IT'S A PART OF ME THAT I SHARE WITH THOSE I CARE FOR."

MIDGET NECKTIE

PUBLISHED ON JUNE 30, 1937

In *The Kansas City Star* that day:

In New York City an elevator falls 16 stories, injuring 26 people.

President and Mrs. Roosevelt attend the wedding of their son, Franklin, Jr., to Ethel du Pont.

In Lexington, Missouri, Josie Mae Grass, a 380-pound "former fat woman in a carnival side show" was shot and killed by her common law husband.

In the nation's capital, the senate conducts hearings on the Memorial Day riot in Chicago involving striking laborers and police in which seven strikers were shot in the back and killed.

Block Size:
5" & 2" finished

Quilt Size:
63" x 70"

Print fabric needed for large and small neckties; 1/2 yard each of 2 reds, 2 blues, 2 greens, 1 rust and 1/2 yard of coordinating background fabric each of 2 reds, 2 blues, 2 greens and 1 rust. (This includes the fabric needed for the striped border and binding.) For the sashing and outer border, 3 yards of fabric are required and for the backing you need 4 1/4 yards.

You will need a total of forty-six 5" finished necktie blocks and fifty-six 2" finished necktie blocks. The small ties are in the sashing and the large ties are put together using 6 blocks across the quilt and 7 blocks the length of the quilt with sashing in between. You will have 4 large ties remaining for each corner of the quilt.

For the borders, cut four 6" x 72" strips on the straight grain of the light background fabric. Set these aside for the outer border. Next cut one 2 1/2" strip from all of the prints and coordinated backgrounds for the neckties for a total of 14 strips. Cut the strips into 5 1/2" rectangles. You should have a total of 98 rectangles. 96 are actually used in the quilt.

For the sashing, which includes the 2" finished midget neckties, cut ninety-seven 2 1/2" x 5 1/2" rectangles from the remaining background fabric. Cut one-hundred and twelve 1 1/2" squares

for the backgrounds of the 2" ties. Cut a 1 1/2" strip from each of your prints. Select one and cut one more strip. Cut the strips into 1 1/2" squares for a total of 112 squares. Cut one 1" strip from each of the fabrics and cut each strip into 1" squares. You will need two 1" squares for each block that will match the 1 1/2" squares.

For the 5" finished neckties, cut one 3" strip from each of your prints. Select one of the prints and cut one more strip so you will have a total of 8 strips. Cut the strips into 3" squares. You will need 92 squares. From the coordinating background fabrics, cut the same number and size of strips and cut into 3" squares. From the necktie prints, cut one 2" strip of each plus one strip of the fabric selected to reuse. Cut the strips into 2" squares. You will need 92 squares.

To piece the neckties, use the flip and stitch method.

Draw a diagonal line on the wrong side of the small print squares. Place a small print square on the corner of a large background square with the right sides together. Stitch on the drawn line. Trim 1/4" from the seam as shown.

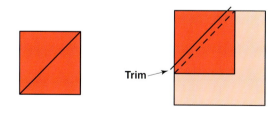

Trim

Press toward the corner. Stitch a large print square and a corner unit together as shown.

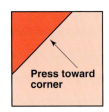

Press toward corner

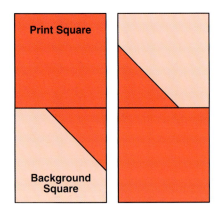

Print Square

Background Square

Stitch another corner unit to a square. Sew the two rows together to make the necktie block as shown.

Make 46 of the 5" finished necktie blocks and 56 of the 2" finished necktie blocks. Set 4 of the 5" blocks aside for the corners of the border. Arrange the 5" blocks in rows. Stitch a 2 1/2" x 5 1/2" sashing strip in between the blocks as shown.

Stitch the small neckties and sashing strips together in horizontal rows. Attach the sashing strips to each row.

Stitch the inner border rectangles together for the sides of the quilt. Twenty-six per side were used on this quilt. Stitch the top and bottom inner border rectangles together and add a necktie block to the ends. Measure the quilt top. Stitch the outer border to the sides of the quilt, then add the top and bottom border.

Layer the backing, the batting and the top together and baste. Quilt as you wish and add the binding to finish the quilt.

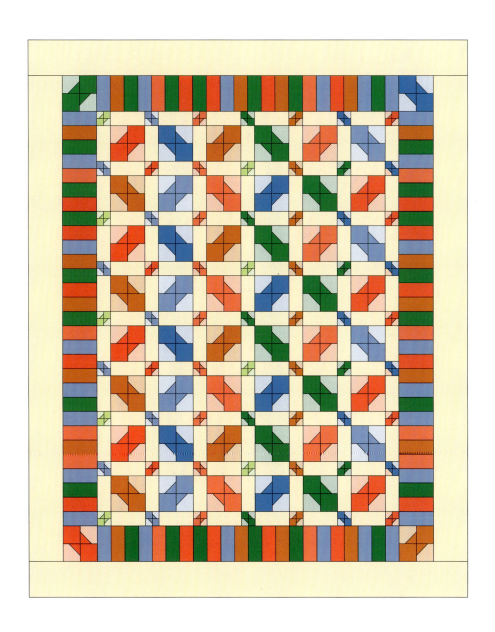

Prairie Point
SHAWNEE, KANSAS

Carol Kirchhoff tells a story that perfectly captures the essence of quilting. It's an intensely personal story. But then quilting is an intensely personal craft.

"I worked at the Attic Window Quilt Shop in Overland Park for 7 years, from 1986 to 1993," Carol begins. "Two wonderful women, Kathy Schamberger and Marilyn McLeod, were co-owners of the store while I was there. Both were diagnosed with serious illnesses in the same year, so they decided to close the shop. Years later, Kathy was killed in an automobile accident. At the funeral, I was talking to her husband and he asked me if I would finish quilting a baby quilt Kathy had started making for their grown daughter who was expecting a child. I said that I certainly would.

"The next week I went to his house to pick up the quilt and instead of a baby quilt, Kathy had been working on a queen size double wedding ring quilt for her daughter's fifth anniversary. I was a bit surprised to say the least. He asked me if I still wanted to work on the quilt. I told him it was an honor to be asked to finish Kathy's quilt because I respected and admired her so much.

"I had never done a quilt of that size and I worried it would take me years to complete. The huge quilt top looked overwhelming. I took it home that night and tried to figure out what to do. That's when I had the idea to ask the women who had worked with Kathy at the Attic Window to help me.

"So I called them up and each was touched to be asked to work on the quilt. Some of us had not seen each other for some time and it was great to get together to baste the

PRAIRIE POINT
7341 QUIVIRA
SHAWNEE, KANSAS 66216
PHONE: 913-268-3333
FAX: 913-268-5606
WEB ADDRESS: WWW.PRAIRIEPOINT.COM
E-MAIL: PRAIRIEPTQUILTS@AOL.COM
ESTABLISHED IN 1995
OVER 3,200 BOLTS OF FABRIC
15 EMPLOYEES

SHAWNEE

quilt. Each one of us took the quilt for a month or so and quilted on it whenever we could. About 8 months later it came back to me. There was still about half of it to be quilted.

"Thank goodness for moms. My mother had told me that she was wanting a project to work on and I just happened to have this quilt that need-

yes, the love in this story are the same qualities that - according to its customers - characterize the Prairie Point quilt shop in Shawnee, Kansas.

Carol Kirchhoff, who has managed Prairie Point since 1999, recently purchased the store.

For Sarah Cullins, a long time customer, this is good news, because it means that the shop will

comments. "We've worked hard to customize our service. We try to offer different levels of service depending on skill and interest, whether you work by hand or machine, whether you're a 'topper' or you like the quilting part."

Carol confesses that she, herself, is a "topper." "Like lots of other quilters, the part I like best is

"IF YOU REALLY WANT TO HELP YOUR CUS-TOMERS YOU HAVE TO GET TO KNOW THEM. AND TO GET TO KNOW THEM YOU HAVE TO LIS-TEN, REALLY LISTEN, TO THEM."

"WOMEN WILL GO THROUGH DIFFERENT CRAFTING FADS BUT ONCE THEY START QUILTING THEY TEND TO STAY WITH IT. THERE'S SOMETHING MORE SUBSTANTIAL AND LASTING ABOUT QUILTING."

ed quilting. So she took it home and finished it. We then gave it back to Kathy's husband to give to their daughter. Steve and his daughter were very grateful.

"Quilts have a way of bringing people together. While I was quilting on Kathy's quilt, I would think of how she influenced my life and what a difference she made in the world. I think that's one of the ways quilts are important. They keep us connected to the memories of people, places and special events in our lives."

The graciousness, generosity, hard work, and,

continue to provide the same level of quality service it's been known for. "Carol is so helpful," says Sarah. "She and her staff are so knowl-edgeable and they really go out of their way to understand your needs."

Sally Kennedy, another loyal Prairie Point shop-per, echoes this sentiment. "The folks there have really created a wonderful environment," Sally explains. "It kind of feels like home. They'll help you solve fabric and color problems. They offer great classes. Plus they all really like to have fun. Whenever I'm there we're always laughing."

Carol smiles when she hears Sarah's and Sally's

selecting and matching the fabric and putting the patterns together," she admits. "After that part is done, I find myself eager to start another project. That's one of the nice things about owning a shop. I'm surrounded by all this great fabric.

"But the best thing is I'm surrounded by all these great people."

Prairie Point
SHAWNEE, KANSAS

VONDA NELSON (ABOVE) FOUNDED
PRAIRIE POINT QUILT SHOP IN
1995 AND WAS ITS SOLE OWNER
UNTIL ITS RECENT SALE TO CAROL
KIRCHHOFF.

IN 1964, WHEN VONDA'S GREAT-
GRANDMOTHER DIED, THE FAMILY
DISCOVERED THAT SHE HAD MADE
AND THEN STORED EIGHT FINISHED
QUILTS, 38 FINISHED QUILT TOPS,
AND BLOCKS FOR 20 MORE QUILTS,
IN A TRUNK IN HER BASEMENT.
WHEN VONDA'S MOTHER DIED IN
1991, VONDA INHERITED THE QUILT
TOPS. THIS TREASURE WAS INSTRU-
MENTAL IN DEEPENING HER LOVE
AND RESPECT FOR QUILTING, AND
FOR THE TALENTS, THE EXCEPTION-
AL GIFTS, OF QUILTERS.

"ONE OF THE JOYS OF THIS SHOP,"
VONDA SAYS, "HAS BEEN GETTING
TO KNOW THE INDIVIDUAL STORIES,
TASTES, AND GOALS OF THE QUIL-
TERS WHO SHOP HERE."

THAT, IN FACT, HAS BEEN THE
GUIDING PRINCIPLE AT PRAIRIE
POINT FROM THE BEGINNING.

THE STAFF OF PRAIRIE POINT. SEATED, FROM LEFT TO RIGHT: SUSAN JARSULIC, KATHY DELANEY, CAROLYN MORE, NAN RUWE, LINDA
POTTER, NANCY NUNN. STANDING, FROM LEFT TO RIGHT: CAROL KIRCHHOFF, VONDA NELSON, PAT MOORE, ALICE SCOTT, BETTY MCNEILL,
JUDY OBERKROM, KELLY ASHTON, DEBI SCHRADER, CONNIE COFFMAN, BARBARA FIFE.

SHAWNEE, KANSAS
Make a Day of it

Shawnee got its start on a river, as did many Midwestern cities and towns. French explorer M. Debourgemont settled the area south of the Kansas River in 1724. As the city grew to its current population of more than 50,000, Shawnee has spread out geographically to the east, south and as a portion of the western boundary of the greater Kansas City area.

Not too far from the bright lights and neon signs of its big city neighbor, citizens of suburban Shawnee and the surrounding Johnson County, Kansas, area appreciate their history while offering all that a 21st century community can provide.

For more information, contact (888) 550-SCVB or www.shawneekschamber.org. It is always best to call ahead to check hours and days of operation for any destination.

WHAT TO SEE AND DO

The Wonderscope Children's Museum fascinates current and former children with the hands-on television studio weather station, hospital operating room and a tornado maker.

5705 Flint, from Prairie Point, drive north on Quivira Road past Johnson Drive to 57th Street, turn east (right) to Flint. Admission charged, (913) 268-8130.

When you think "museum," chances are, "totally wired" does not come to mind. It will at the Johnson County Museum of History, where one of the exhibits is the 1950s All-Electric House. See this and other exhibits, artifacts and photographs of Johnson County's past.

6305 Lackman, from Prairie Point, drive north on Quivira Road, then turn west (left) on Shawnee Mission Parkway, past Pflumm to the Lackman Road exit, turn north (right) to the museum. Admission charged, (913) 631-6709, http://kcsun4.kcstar.com/schools/JohnsonCounty Museums/index.htm.

Old Shawnee Town, in the heart of modern day Shawnee, is a stroll down the wooden sidewalks of the Western frontier. The town combines original buildings dating from as early as1843 with replicated building from the 1800s and 1900s. Exhibits, artifacts and gardens complete today's peek into Shawnee's frontier past.

57th and Cody, from Prairie Point, drive north on Quivira Road past Johnson Drive to 57th Street, turn east (right) to Cody. Admission charged, (913) 248-2360.

OTHER JOHNSON COUNTY, KANSAS, ATTRACTIONS

Deanna Rose Children's Farmstead, 138th Street and Switzer, Overland Park, Kan., (913) 895-6350, www.opprf.org/Farm.htm

Legler Barn Museum, 14907 W. 87th St., Lenexa, Kan., (913) 492-0038, ci.lenexa.ks.us/cityhall/parks/leglerbarn.html

Mahaffie Farmstead and Stagecoach Stop, 1101 Old Kansas City Road, Olathe, Kan., (913) 782-6972

Shawnee Indian Mission State Historic Site, 3403 W. 53rd, Fairway, Kan., (913) 262-0867, www.kshs.org/places/shawnmis.htm

THE NEW KANSAS SPEEDWAY IS IN NEIGHBORING WYANDOTTE COUNTY

LOCAL FLAVOR

Rainforest Cafe brings the outdoors in, the rainforest far north of the equator, and food for all ages to your table.

Lower level of Oak Park Mall, 11327 W. 95th Street, from Prairie Point, drive south on Quivira Road to 95th, turn east (left) and enter the mall parking lot, (913) 438-7676.

First Watch serves a touch of class with their breakfast, brunch and lunch creations. This location is one of several in the Kansas City area.

11112 Shawnee Mission Parkway, from Prairie Point, drive north on Quivira Road to Shawnee Mission Parkway, turn right (east), (913) 631-0888.

Mezzaluna has been praised in Zagat Survey for its "fantastic interpretations of Northern Italian cuisine."

7807 Quivira Road, from Prairie Point, drive five blocks south on Quivira Road and turn east (left), (913) 248-0087, www.mezzaluna.com.

Make a night of it

At White Haven Motor Lodge, chances are you'll be greeted by the owners. They keep service and comfort in mind, with refrigerators in every room, a free continental breakfast, handicapped rooms and an outdoor pool.

8039 Metcalf Avenue, from Prairie Point, drive south on Quivira Road, then take I-435 east to the Metcalf exit, turn north (left) and drive to 81st Street. White Haven is on the east (right), (913) 649-8200, www.white-haven.com.

Besides comfortable rooms, Wyndham Garden Hotel has a restaurant, pool, lounge and free breakfast. It is conveniently located on the northeast corner of I-435 and Metcalf in Overland Park, Kan.

7000 W. 108th Street, Overland Park, Kan., from Prairie Point, drive south on Quivira Road, then take I-435 east to the Metcalf exit, turn north (left), move to the far right lane, pass under I-435, then turn east (right) on 108th Street, (800) 996-3426 or (913) 383-2550, e-mail: overlandpark@wyndham.com.

You can camp in the city, at Walnut Grove RV Park in Merriam, Kan. It's a popular place, so call during the day to make reservations.

10218 Johnson Drive, from Prairie Point, drive north on Quivira Road to Johnson Drive, then east (right) on Johnson Drive past Nieman Road. Walnut Grove RV Park is on the north (left) side of Johnson Drive, approximately one-half mile west of I-35, (913) 262-3023.

—Lori Wilson

PRAIRIE POINT
7341 QUIVIRA
SHAWNEE,
KANSAS 66216
913-268-3333

WINGED SQUARE
PUBLISHED ON OCTOBER 20, 1937

In *The Kansas City Star* that day:

In Topeka, Alf Landon received scores of telegrams congratulating him on his radio speech criticizing President Franklin Roosevelt's New Deal policies.

In Dexter, Kansas, a mystery is solved. Residents had reported a man dumping a body in a creek on the outskirts of town. Turns out the "body" was just an old vacuum cleaner disposed of by a traveling salesman who'd taken it in on trade for a new one he'd sold to a Dexter housewife.

A pack train of horses and mules was used to recover 19 bodies from a mountainside airplane crash in Utah.

Sixty-five more people are executed in Russia for "anti-Soviet" activities, bringing the total known killings to 527 over a five-month period.

PIECED BY CAROL KIRCHHOFF.
QUIK STITCHED BY LINDA POTTER.

SEE OTHER QUILTS BASED ON THIS PATTERN ON PAGES 68-73.

Block Size:
9" finished

Quilt size:
51" x 51"

Fabric needed: 1/2 yard each of 6 different greens, 3 yards of blue for blocks, alternating blocks, settings and corner triangles, 1/2 yard of one of the greens for binding, 3 1/4 yards for backing.

From each of the green prints, cut three 3 1/2" squares. (You will have 2 squares left over.)

Cut six strips 2 1/2" x 42" using the extra 1/2 yard of green fabric. These strips will be used for the binding.

From the blue print, cut thirty-two 3 1/2" squares, four 14 1/2" squares and eight 9 1/2" squares for alternating blocks.

Cut 2 of the 14 1/2" squares diagonally two times as shown making quarter-square triangles. These are the setting triangles of which you need eight.

Cut the remaining two 14 1/2" squares diagonally as shown. These are the corner triangles of which you need four.

Choose the half-square triangle piecing method you wish to use and cut the units according to the instructions.

Method 1. *Triangles on a Roll TM*

From each of the 6 green prints, cut one 10" x 20" strip. From the blue print, cut six 10" x 20" strips. (The blue fabric can, of course, be cut from selvage edge to selvage edge and then trimmed to a length of 20." You will only need three strips if you do this.)

When using *Triangles on a Roll TM*, you will need to count 32 square units of paper for each green print. Follow the instructions given with the *Triangles on a Roll TM*.

Method 2. Rotary cutting instructions.

From each of the six green prints cut two 2 3/8" x 42" strips from selvage to selvage edge. From the blue print, cut twelve 2 3/8" x 42" strips from selvage to selvage edge. Layer each blue strip with a green strip with the right sides facing. Press. Trim off the selvages and cut the strips into 2 3/8" squares. Draw a diagonal line from corner to corner on the wrong side of the blue square and stitch 1/4" on either side of the line. Cut on the drawn line. Open each square and press towards the green print. You will need 384 of these half-square triangle units.

You will need to make 16 blocks for this quilt.

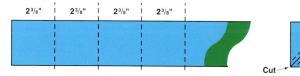

To assemble the block:

Sew 8 half-square triangle units together as shown. Make 2 rows like this and set aside.

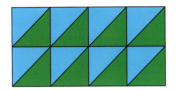

Now sew 4 half-square triangles together as shown. Make two of these rows and set aside.

For the top row of the block, stitch a row of 8 half-square triangles to one blue square as shown.

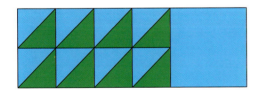

For the middle row, sew a row of 4 half-square triangles to the left side of a green square. Turn the remaining row of 4 half-square triangles and sew them to the right side of the green square as shown.

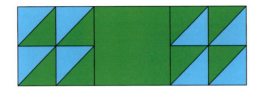

For the bottom row, sew a blue square to a row of 8 half-square triangles that have been turned as shown.

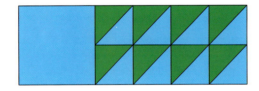

Sew the three rows together to complete the block.

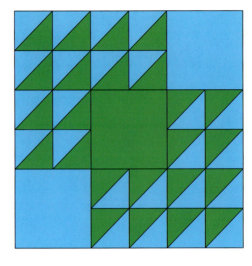

To assemble the quilt, sew the pieced blocks and the side triangles together in diagonal rows as shown. Sew the corner triangles to the quilt top. Trim the excess fabric from the side and corner triangles, leaving a 1/4" seam allowance beyond the corners of each block. Layer the backing, batting and top. Baste the layers together, quilt and bind the edges to complete the quilt.

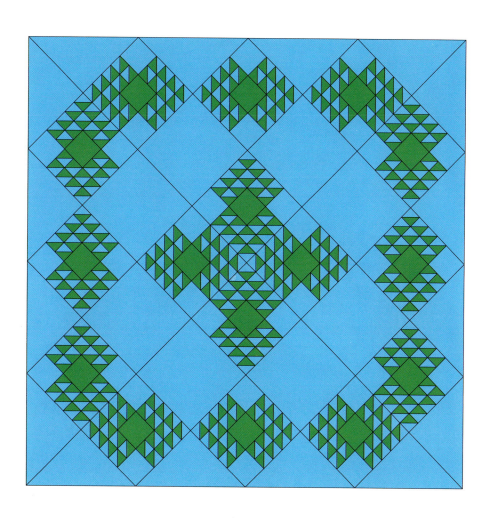

Liberty Quilt Shop
LIBERTY, MISSOURI

Julie Kiffin has a keen eye. She knows a valuable quilt when she sees one. And she's seen plenty. Julie owns the Liberty Quilt Shop, in Liberty, Missouri, where hundreds of quilts of exceptional quality and beauty have been created. She's assisted her customers in understanding and appreciating quilts they've inherited or purchased, and in making heirloom quilts of their own to pass on to future generations. Eventually she expects to exploit her experience and training by becoming a professional quilt appraiser.

Yet Julie knows that the value of a quilt is measured in more than dollars and cents. She knows that every quilt has stitched into it a priceless story. *This quilt was made the winter the twins were born. That quilt was made when brother was off fighting the war. And the churchwomen made that one over there after Mom died.*

"I have no talent for quilt design," Julie claims. "But, I'm good at researching design and fabric history. And I especially enjoy learning the stories behind specific quilts. I try to encourage quilters and people who own quilts to learn as much as they can about their quilts and to keep written records. When there are no records of a quilt's history, it becomes a mystery. I'd like to become knowledgeable enough about fabric and design to help solve some of those quilt mysteries."

Julie first enrolled in a quilting class for a very practical reason. She wanted to make a quilt for a bed. .

These days Julie quilts, in part, for reasons a bit more intellectual. It's a way for her to learn about the lives of women of earlier generations.

LIBERTY QUILT SHOP
131 S. WATER, LIBERTY, MO 64068
816-781-7966
WEB ADDRESS:
WWW.LIBERTYQUILTSHOP.COM
E-MAIL: LIBERTYQLT@AOL.COM
ESTABLISHED: 1991
BOLTS OF FABRIC: OVER 4,000
EMPLOYEES: 10

LIBERTY

"In a sense, women journaled through their quilting," she explains. "Quilting has always been a way for women to create a lasting personal expression of themselves. Quilting is a way of studying their lives. It puts me in touch with my roots, as a woman."

But Julie also quilts because it puts her in touch with women of younger generations.

"The social reasons are probably most important," she says. "I've always wanted a daughter. So I tend to collect surrogate daughters, including my nieces, and my young quilting friends. The shop is a place for me to be a part of the lives of younger women."

Customers at the Liberty Quilt Shop confirm that Julie tends to "adopt" those special to her. Jean Warder had been a long time quilter but had drifted away from the craft over time. Then she attended an open house at Julie's shop.

"She got me back into it," Jean explains. "First of all, the store has wonderful products, so it's a joy to shop there. But mostly, it's Julie and her staff. They know you and remember what's important to you. And Julie makes you feel as if you're her favorite customer."

While the camaraderie that she shares with her customers is the primary benefit of being a quilt shop owner, Julie reports that there are other joys to be had.

"I just love the fabric," she says. "I'm a very tactile person. I really enjoy handling the material. And, of course, it's wonderful to look at."

Quilt historian and author Barbara Brackman believes that the Liberty Quilt Shop has one of the finest selections of fabric in the Midwest.

"Julie Kiffin and her staff have really created a unique palate of patterns and colors," she states. "They specialize in the 'primitive' look. And quilters from all over the region have made the store a destination."

Julie jokes about the fabric envy she detects among some of her customers. "I think some of them are hanging around because they hope to inherit my fabric collection when I die."

Humor and kindness are Julie's trademarks. Jean Warder says that when her husband became ill, Julie extended herself in surprising ways. "It just shows how a quilt shop is a different kind of place," she explains. "You'd never see your pharmacist or your dry cleaner providing the kind of emotional support I got from Julie and the people at her store."

When asked about her role as customer caregiver Julie will only say "It's no more than they've all done for me."

Liberty Quilt Shop
LIBERTY, MO

THE LIBERTY QUILT SHOP STAFF.
LEFT TO RIGHT: AMBER COFFEY, CAROL BOX,
DONNA BOGUE, SHARON DONEGAN, SHOP MANAGER,
JO CRABB. NOT PICTURED: JEAN FISHER, DORLA
KENWORTHY, JENNIFER KOOISTRA, JUDY LOVELL,
KATHY MOORE, ANN O'DELL, AND JACQUE ZINK.

"QUILTING IS A WAY OF CARING FOR FAMILY
AND FRIENDS. THERE'S A RICH HISTORY OF
WOMEN SUPPORTING EACH OTHER THROUGH
QUILTS AND QUILTING."

The history of Liberty began with the business of outfitting westward pioneers. Today, the business of Liberty is its history. It is the home of one of Missouri's oldest private colleges, William Jewell College. The city's architecture from the 1800s is preserved with more than 30 buildings listed on the National Register of Historic Places. Some are in Liberty's original business district.

Liberty has successfully revitalized its old downtown, especially its town square. If those buildings could talk, they'd tell you stories —

true stories of Liberty's struggle during the Civil War, as well as the first daylight bank robbery. Instead, museums preserve these and other stories, with details from knowledgeable people.

For more information, contact Clay County Visitors Bureau at (816) 792-7691 or www.clay-county.com, or the Liberty Chamber of Commerce at (816) 781-5200 or www.libertychamber.com. It is always best to call ahead to check hours and days of operation for any destination.

WHAT TO SEE AND DO

A take of $60,000 doesn't seem like a big heist now, but it was in 1866, when the Jesse James gang was reportedly committed the first daylight bank robbery. The bank office is so authentically restored that you'll check over your shoulder for masked men while you visit Jesse James Bank Museum.

103 North Water, two blocks north of Liberty Quilt Shop, admission charged, (816) 781-4458.

———————

The Historic Liberty Jail is known for its most famous prisoner, Joseph Smith, Jr. He and other members of the Church of Jesus Christ of Latter Day Saints were imprisoned for their beliefs. The 1833 jail was reconstructed by the church in 1963.

216 North Main, three blocks north and one block west of Liberty Quilt Shop, admission free, (816) 781-3188.

———————

Martha Lafite Thompson Nature Sanctuary is a peaceful 100-acre setting with an old growth forest, nature hiking, an interpretive center and outdoor activities.

407 North LaFrenz, from Liberty Quilt Shop, drive east on Mill to the second stop light, turn east (right) at William Jewell College, cross the railroad tracks and continue one-half mile to LaFrenz Road, admission charged only for groups of 10 or more, (816) 781-8598.

———————

Jesse James Farm and Museum (pictured right) 21216 Jesse James Farm Road Kearney, MO (816) 628-6065. (Just up the road from Liberty.)

LOCAL FLAVOR

Besides its namesake dish, Luckee's Pizza also creates pasta, Italian sandwiches, appetizers and salads.

6 East Franklin, two blocks north and one block west of Liberty Quilt Shop (816) 781-3333, e-mail: luckees@earthlink.net.

———————

Fork 'N Spoon Café is mom-and-pop and more. Order a home-cooked breakfast, lunch or dinner anytime, day or night. The "and more" are the

**LIBERTY QUILT SHOP
131 S. WATER, LIBERTY, MO 64068
816-781-7966**

weekend specials — prime rib, catfish and shrimp scampi. Other features are kids' meals and lighter appetite choices.

12 West Kansas, one block north and two blocks west of Liberty Quilt Shop, (816) 792-0707.

A century ago it was a hardware store. Now it's the Hardware Café, with more than a decade of delicious service. Its American cuisine has been recognized for excellence by USA Today and Zagat Survey.

5 East Kansas, one block north and one block west of Liberty Quilt Shop, (816) 792-3500, www.thehardwarecafe.com.

MAKE A NIGHT OF IT

The James Inn is a bed & breakfast, as well as a day spa. The restored church, built in 1913, is highlighted by Gothic windows. Relax in a jacuzzi tub or work out in the exercise room.

342 North Water Street, three and a half blocks north of Liberty Quilt Shop, (816) 781-3677, www.thejamesinn.com.

At Hampton Inn, you'll find large hotel features and small inn ambiance. Wake up to a complimentary breakfast. Enjoy the indoor pool and fully-equipped fitness center.

8551 North Church Road, from Liberty Quilt Shop, drive two blocks west to Gallatin and one block north to Kansas, then take Kansas west. Kansas will become Highway 152. Cross I-35, then take a right at the first stop light. (800) HAMPTON or (816) 415-9600.

Camping is available at Miller's Camp Park, conveniently located at I-35 and Highway152. Reservations required.

145 1/2 Stewart Road, from Liberty Quilt Shop, drive two blocks west to Gallatin and one block north to Kansas, then take Kansas west. Kansas will become Highway 152. Cross I-35 and Miller's Camp Park on the northwest corner of I-35 and Highway 152, (816) 781-7724.

—Lori Wilson

Annual Events
LIBERTY, MISSOURI

In May, Spring on the Square, (816) 792-6000, Ext. 3038

In June, Liberty Gathering, (816) 792-3670

In September, Liberty Fall Festival, (816) 781-5200

In October, Trick or Treat on the Square, (816) 781-5200

In November, Historic Holiday Homes Tour, (816) 792-1849

In December, Santa Arrives on the Square, (816) 781-5200

ABOVE: CHILDREN HIKING AT THE MARTHA LAFITE THOMPSON NATURE SANCTUARY.

ROSE DREAM
PUBLISHED ON
DECEMBER 27, 1930

In *The Kansas City Star* that day:

Steel mills in Youngstown, Ohio, call 2,000 workers back to work after an extended lay off.

Over 100 men and boys who had been ice fishing on Lake Erie are temporarily stranded when a huge ice floe breaks away.

Prince George, youngest son of Great Britain's King George, is thrown from his horse during a fox hunt and is hospitalized with minor injuries.

Thomas Edison gives the pope a dictation machine as a Christmas present. The pontiff is said to highly prize the gift.

Block Size:
13" finished

Large Quilt: 78" x 91"

Fabric needed: 5 yards background fabric

Twenty-one 1/3 yard cuts of prints (This will give you enough fabric to make 2 blocks from each print.)

3/4 yard for binding

6 yards for backing

Trace templates given onto template plastic and include the seam allowance. Either mark the pieces directly onto the fabric and cut out using scissors or use a small rotary cutter to cut around the templates.

Pin and sew a print and background piece on the curve. Clip the seam allowance along the curve and press towards the larger piece. Set aside.

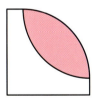

Sew a 2" background square to each short side of a matching print as shown. Press toward the print. Pin and sew the two units together to make 1/4 of the block as shown.

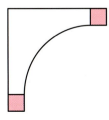

Make another section just like this.

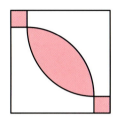

Reverse the fabric and make the other two sections of the block as shown.

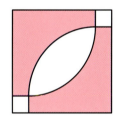

Sew two sections together as shown.

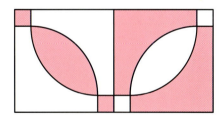

Sew the next two sections together as shown.

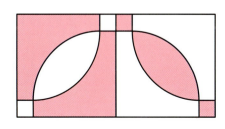

PIECED BY NAIDA McKEE.
QUILTED BY DENISE HESTER.

Sew the two strips together to complete the block.

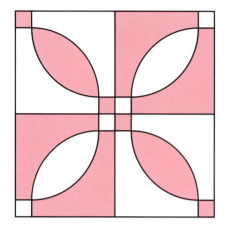

You will need 42 blocks (6 blocks across and 7 blocks down) to make the full size quilt.

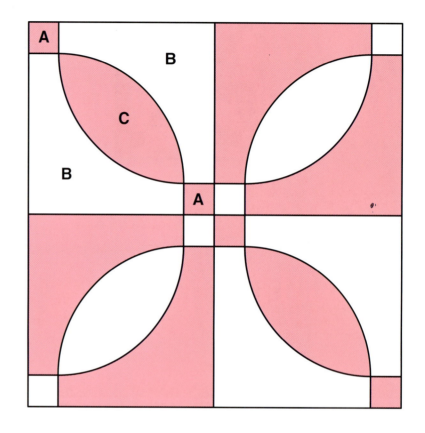

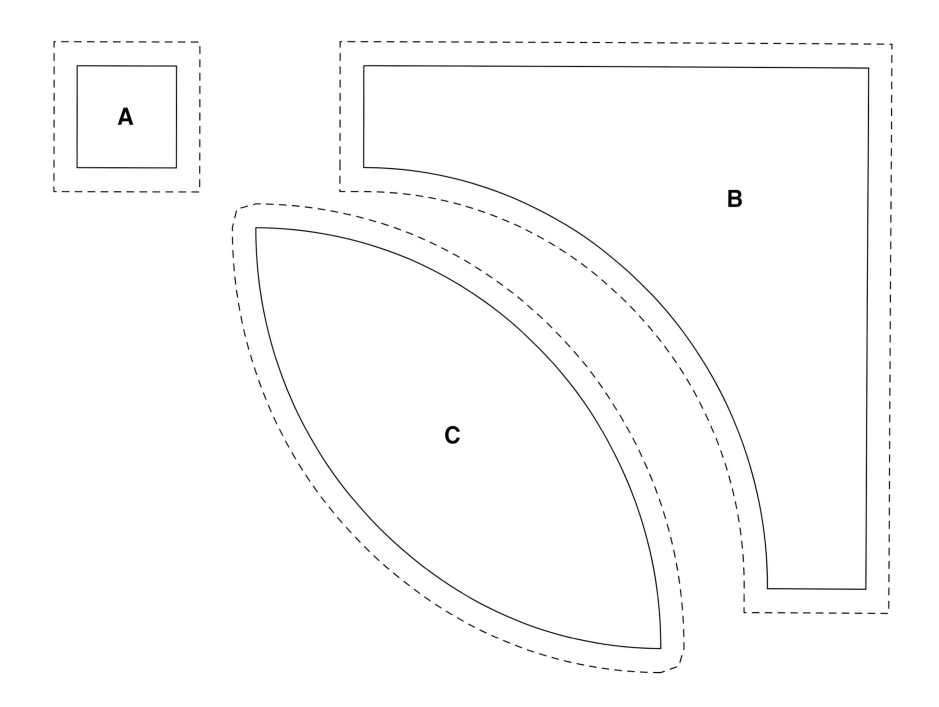

QUILT GALLERY *Additional Quilts from Kansas City Quiltmakers*

GARY'S LITTLE GRANDMA BOWTIE

Quilt Block: 6"
Finished

Quilt Size: 82" x 98"

Fabric needed: background and border - 3 1/2 yards; prints - 4 1/2 yards; binding - 3/4 yards; backing - 6 yards.

From the background fabrics, cut 3 1/2" squares. You need 368 squares. From the print fabrics, cut 3 1/2" squares. Make sure to have pairs of these. You need a total of 368 squares or 184 pairs. Also from the print fabrics, cut 2" squares. You will also need a total of 184 pairs. These pairs should match the 3 1/2" square cut from the prints.

Arrange the blocks in rows. Stitch the rows together. Sew on the side borders. Sew the pieced blocks to both ends of the top and bottom border strips. Sew these to the quilt to finish the top.

Quilt and bind the top as you desire.

PIECED BY JEANNE POORE.
MACHINE QUILTED BY FREDA SMITH.

Amish Style Midget Necktie Quilt

Block Size:
7 1/2" finished

Quilt Size: 68" x 68"

Fabric needed: 3 1/2 yards black background fabric, including setting blocks, borders and binding. 1/3 yards each of red, blue, green, pink, rose and yellow solids for large and small ties and 4 1/8 yards for the backing.

From background fabric, cut four 8" wide strips for the large inner border. Set aside. Cut twelve 8" setting squares; seventy-two 2" squares; eight 2" x 40" strips (4 for the outer narrow border and 4 for the binding); 68 rectangles 2" x 3 1/2" for block piecing; one-hundred and thirty six 2" squares for block piecing and thirty-four 1 1/4" squares for the small neckties in the center of each block.

From each of the purple and rose fabric, cut thirty-two 2" squares, forty 1 1/4" squares, eight 3/4" squares and one 2" x 40" strip subcut into 2" squares for the outer pieced border.

From the pink fabric, cut twenty-four 2" squares, thirty 1 1/4" squares, 6 - 3/4" squares and one 2" x 40" strip subcut into 2" squares for the outer pieced border.

From each of the yellow, green and blue fabric, cut sixteen 2" squares, twenty 1 1/4" squares, four 3/4" squares and one 2" strip subcut into 2" squares for the outer pieced border.

To piece the blocks, follow the general stitch and flip instructions for this pattern. Each 7 1/2"

finished block contains 4 pieced 3" neckties, 1 pieced 1 1/2" necktie and 4 sashing units.

Make 4 blocks of the purple, 4 of the rose, 3 of the pink and 2 each of blue, yellow and green.

Stitch the block together as shown with a 2" x 3 1/2" black sashing strip between the neckties. You need two rows. Be sure the ties point to the outside corners of the block.

For the center row, sew a sashing strip to the left and the right of each small necktie block as shown.

Sew the three rows together to complete the block.

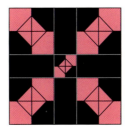

Layout the 13 pieced quilt blocks and 12 solid setting blocks as diagrammed. Sew together in rows. Measure the quilt top. Cut the 4 strips of 8" wide border fabric the length of the quilt measurement. Stitch the two side borders on first. Stitch the four pieced corner blocks to the ends of the top and bottom 8" wide border strips then sew them to the quilt.

Sew the 2" black and colored squares together in strips and stitch them to the sides, bottom and top of the quilt. Sew the 2" black outer border to the sides, bottom and top of the quilt. Your quilt is now ready to baste, quilt and bind.

WINGS OF RED (WINGED SQUARE)

Block Size:
12" finished

Quilt Size: 67" x 85"

Fabric Needed: 1/2 yard each of 12 different reds for blocks; 6 3/4 yards of beige for blocks, setting and corner triangles; 2/3 yard of red print for binding; and 5 1/2 yards for backing.

The quilt is made up of 31 winged square blocks.

From each of the 12 red print fabrics, cut three 4 1/2" squares. From one of the red prints, cut eight 2 1/2" x 42" strips for binding.

From the beige print, cut sixty-two 4 1/2" squares for the pieced blocks. Cut five 18 1/2" squares. Cut 3 of these squares diagonally twice making quarter square triangles. Although you will have 12 of these, you will only use 10. Cut the other 2 squares diagonally making 4 large triangles. These are for the corners.

Choose either the *Triangles on a Roll TM* or the rotary cutting method for making half-square triangles.

Using the *Triangles on a roll TM* method:

From each of the 12 red prints cut two 6" x 42" strips from selvage edge to selvage edge. Remember to remove the selvages before sewing.

From the beige print, cut twenty-four 6" x 42" strips.

You will need to count 31 square units of paper for each red print. Follow the instructions given with the *Triangles on a Roll TM*.

Using the rotary cutting method:

From each of the 12 red prints, cut three 2 7/8" x 42" strips. From the beige print, cut thirty-six 2 7/8" x 42" strips.

With right sides together layer the 2 7/8" x 42" red strips and the 2 7/8" x 42" beige strips in pairs. Trim off the selvages and press. Cut the layered strips into 2 7/8" squares. You should have 372 of the pairs. Draw a diagonal line from corner to corner on the wrong side of each beige square. Sew 1/4" on each side of the line. Cut on the drawn line. Open each square and press towards the red prints. You need to make 744 of the red/beige half-square triangle units.

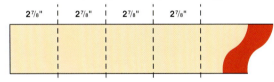

Cut →

Assemble the blocks. You will need 31 blocks.

To assemble the quilt, sew the pieced blocks and the side triangles together in diagonal rows. Sew the corner triangles to the quilt top and trim the excess fabric from the side and corner triangles, making sure to allow a 1/4" seam allowance beyond the corners of each block.

Layer the backing, batting and top. Baste the layers together and quilt as desired. Complete the quilt by binding the edges.

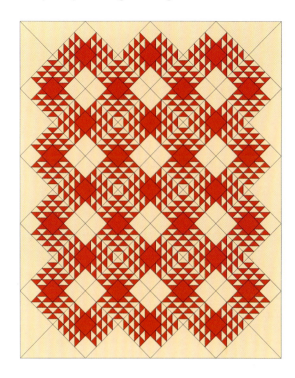

PIECED BY CAROL KIRCHHOFF.
HAND QUILTED BY HELEN BERGSIEKER.

FLORAL WINGS OF SPRING (WINGED SQUARE)

Block Size: 12" finished

Quilt Size: 78" x 94"

Fabric Needed: 2/3 yard each of 5 different greens for blocks; 1/2 yard each of 5 different pinks for blocks; 8 1/4 yards of floral print for plain alternating blocks, side and corner triangles, border and binding; 5/8 yard of green print for inner border; 1/2 yard pink print for middle border and 6 yards for backing.

The quilt is made up of 14 green winged square blocks and 7 pink winged square blocks. It also uses 10 floral print alternating blocks.

From each green print fabric, cut three 4 1/2" squares. From the green border fabric, cut eight 2 1/2" x 42" strips.

From each pink fabric, cut two 4 1/2" squares. From the pink border fabric, cut eight 1 1/2" x 42" strips.

From the floral background fabric, cut twenty-eight 4 1/2" squares for the pieced blocks. Cut ten 12 1/2" squares. Cut five 18 1/2" squares. Cut 3 of these squares diagonally twice making quarter square triangles. Although you will have 12 of these, you will only use 10. Cut the other 2 squares diagonally making 4 large triangles. Cut nine 3 1/2" x 42" strips for the border and nine 2 1/2" x 42" strips for the binding.

Choose either the *Triangles on a Roll TM* or the rotary cutting method for making half-square triangles.

Using the *Triangles on a roll TM* method:

From each of the 5 green prints cut two 6" x 42" strips from selvage edge to selvage edge. Remember to remove the selvages before sewing.

From the floral background, cut ten 6" x 42" strips.

You will need to count 34 square units of paper for each green print.

For the pink combination blocks, you will need to cut one 6" x 42" strip from each pink print fabric. From the floral background, cut five 6" x 42" strips.

You will need to count 17 square units of paper for each pink print. Follow the instructions given with the Triangles on a Roll TM.

Using the rotary cutting method:

From each of the five green prints, cut three 2 7/8" x 42" strips. From the floral background print, cut fifteen 2 7/8" x 42" strips.

From each of the five pink prints, cut two 2 7/8" x 42" strips and from the floral background, cut ten 2 7/8" x 42" strips.

With right sides together layer the 2 7/8" x 42" green or pink strip and the 2 7/8" x 42" floral strip in pairs. Trim off the selvages and press. Cut the layered strips into 2 7/8" squares. You should have 168 of the green/floral pairs and 84 of the pink/floral pairs. Draw a diagonal line from corner to corner on the wrong side of each pink or green square. Sew 1/4" on each side of the line. Cut on the drawn line. You should have a total of 336 green/floral squares and a total of 168 pink/floral squares.

Assemble the blocks. You will make 14 green blocks and 7 pink blocks.

To assemble the quilt, sew the pieced blocks and the side triangles together in diagonal rows. Sew the corner triangles to the quilt top and trim the excess fabric from the side and corner triangles, making sure to allow a 1/4" seam allowance beyond the corners of each block.

Sew the pink inner border to each side, then add the top and bottom strips. Repeat with the green middle border and floral outer border.

Layer the backing, batting and top. Baste the layers together and quilt as desired. Complete the quilt by binding the edges.

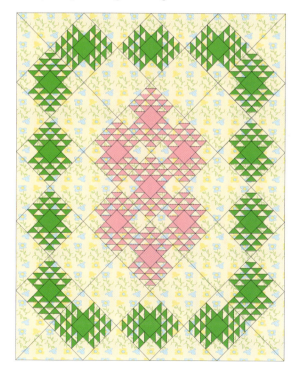

Cut →

PIECED BY CAROL KIRCHHOFF.
MACHINE QUILTED BY JEANNE ZYCK.

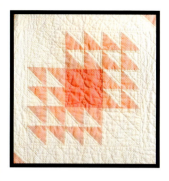

OLD FASHIONED WINGED SQUARE

Block Size: 12" finished

Quilt Size: 72" x 72"

Fabric Needed: 1 3/4 yards of pink for blocks; 1 yard of dark pink for blocks and binding; 4 1/2 yards of white for blocks and alternating blocks and 5 1/2 yards for backing.

The quilt is made up of 20 winged square blocks and 16 alternating blocks.

From dark pink fabric, cut twenty 4 1/2" squares and eight 2 1/2" x 42" strips for binding.

From white fabric, cut sixteen 12 1/2" squares and forty 4 1/2" squares.

Choose either the *Triangles on a Roll TM* or the rotary cutting method for making half-square triangles. You will need 2" finished size.

Using the *Triangles on a roll TM* method:

From the pink fabric cut nine 6" x 42" strips from selvage edge to selvage edge. Remember to remove the selvages before sewing.

From the white fabric, cut nine 6" x 42" strips.

You will need to count 240 square units of paper. Follow the instructions given with the *Triangles on a Roll TM*.

Using the rotary cutting method:

From the pink fabric, cut eighteen 2 7/8" x 42" strips. From the white fabric, cut eighteen 2 7/8" x 42" strips.

With right sides together layer the 2 7/8" x 42" pink strip and the 2 7/8" x 42" white strip in pairs. Trim off the selvages and press. Cut the layered strips into 2 7/8" squares. You should have 240 pairs. Draw a diagonal line from corner to corner on the wrong side of the white square. Sew 1/4" on each side of the line. Cut on the drawn line. Open the squares and press toward the pink. You should have a total of 480 pink and white half-square triangles.

Assemble the blocks. You will need 20 pink and white blocks.

To assemble the quilt, sew the pieced blocks and the alternating white blocks together in rows according to the diagram.

Layer the backing, batting and top. Baste the layers together and quilt as desired. Complete the quilt by binding the edges.

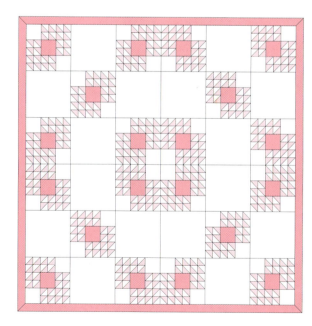

PIECED BY CAROL KIRCHHOFF.
HAND QUILTED BY HELEN BERGSIEKER.

PIECED AND MACHINE QUILTED
BY NANCY DIETZ.

PIECED BY RUTH LOFGREN.
MACHINE QUILTED BY RUTH
LOFGREN AND KARI LANE.

"ARROWHEAD TRELLIS" A VARIATION ON THE ORIGINAL. DESIGNED AND PIECED BY JENISE CANTLON. HANDQUILTED BY JENISE CANTLON. MACHINE QUILTED BY KARI LANE.

PIECED BY JERRY STUBE. MACHINE QUILTED BY KARI LANE.

"SCRAP HAPPY ARROWHEAD"
PIECED AND MACHINE QUILTED
BY BECKY NEAL.

PIECED AND MACHINE QUILTED
BY BECKY NEAL.

MACHINE PIECED AND QUILTED
BY KARI LANE.

ARROWHEAD TABLE RUNNER PIECED
BY CINDY OLIVER. MACHINE QUILTED
BY BONNIE INGRAM.

Additional Quilt Shops
Kansas City Area

Cat's Whiskers
106 W. Maple St.
Independence, MO 64050
(816) 254-1702

Harper's Fabric and Quilt Co.
7917 Santa Fe Drive
Overland Park, KS 66204
(913) 648-2739
www.husqvarnaviking.com

Jenell's Quilt Patch
15510 State Avenue
Basehor, KS 66007
(913) 724-4610

Overbrook Quilt Connections
500 Maple
Overbrook, KS 66524
(888) 665-7841
www.overbrookquilts.com

Peddler's Wagon
115 Main
Parkville, MO 64152
(816) 741-0225

Prairie Pieces
200 W. Main St.
Council Grove, KS 66846
(785) 767-6628

Quilters' Haven
120-B S. Clairborne Road
Olathe, KS 66062
(913) 764-8600
e-mail: quiltershaven@wans.com

Quilters' Paradise
713 8th St.,
Baldwin City, KS 66006
(785) 594-3477
www.grapevine.net/~qparadis

Quilting Bits & Pieces
714 Main
Eudora, KS 66025
(877) 639-2080
www.eudoraks.com

Rustic Yearnings
17601A E. 40 Highway
Independence, MO 64055
(816) 373-2423
www.rusticyearnings.com

Stitchin' Traditions
Holliday Square Shopping Center
3005 S. W. Topeka Blvd.
Topeka, KS 66611
(785) 266-4130

Stitch On Needlework Shop
926 Massachusetts
Lawrence, KS 66044
(800) 989-1101
e-mail: stchon@aol.com